Phases of Faith in the Biblical Story

Sherrill Gardner Stevens

© 2022
Published in the United States by Nurturing Faith Inc., Macon GA,
www.nurturingfaith.net.

Nurturing Faith is the book publishing arm of Good Faith Media (goodfaithmedia.org).

Library of Congress Cataloging-in-Publication Data is available.

ISBN: 978-1-63528-164-4

All rights reserved. Printed in the United States of America.

Contents

Introduction 1
    Patriarchal Period 2
    Tribal Period 2
    Kingdom Period 2
    The Exile Period 3

Old Testament

Chapter 1—Religion in the Patriarchal Period 5
    Abram/Abraham 5
    Isaac 12
    Jacob 14
    Joseph 17

Chapter 2—Religion in the Tribal Period 19
    Joseph's Last Years 19
    The Early Life of Moses 20
    The Preparation of Moses for Leadership 20
    The Contest in Egypt and the Exodus 21
    The Journey to Sinai 23
    The Significance of Sinai 23
    The Origins of Mosaic Religion 25
    The Mosaic Sacrificial System 25
    A Mosaic Summary 28

Chapter 3—Religion in the Kingdom Period 31
    The Reigns of Saul, David, and Solomon 31
    The Divided Kingdom 33
    Religion in a Time of Imperial Change 33
    The Emergence of Monotheism 35

Chapter 4—Religion in the Exile Period 37
    Religious Development 37
    The Influence of Persian Religion 40

New Testament

Chapter 5—Learning from the Life and Teachings of Jesus 43
- Learning from Jesus about God 44
- Learning from Jesus about Ourselves 46
- Learning from Jesus about Salvation 48
- Learning from Jesus about Eternity 52

Chapter 6—Learning from Acts and the Pauline Letters 57
- The Conversion and Inclusion of Paul 59
- The Missionary Spread of Christianity 60
- Paul's Beliefs and Influence 63
- How Paul Differs from Jesus 66

Chapter 7—Learning from the Later New Testament Writings 69
- The Pastoral Epistles 69
- Hebrews 69
- James 70
- 1 Peter 70
- 2 Peter 72
- The Johannine Letters 72
- Jude 74
- The Revelation 74

Chapter 8—Learning from Post-Biblical Changes in Tenets of Faith 77
- "Followers of the Way" Become Churches 78
- Hammering Out the Tenets of Faith 78
- Writings Become Sacred and Canonized 79
- Church Organizations Develop 80
- New Tenets of Faith Develop 81

Conclusion 83
- Sin and Salvation 83
- Religious Rituals 85
- A Disclaimer and an Affirmation 89

To Marguerite Godwin Stevens

Devoted Soulmate
Exemplary Mother
Gifted Teacher

Introduction

In the pages that follow, I will demonstrate through the familiar text of the Bible the development of religious faith, and the practices that express it, from the "call" of Abraham to the traditional Protestant Christian religion since the Reformation of the 16th century CE.

I am a devout "Jesus" theologian who cherishes the Bible deeply, but I do not believe it is a product of verbal inspiration. Our Bible is a product of human response to the issues of life, nature, aspiration, fear, culture, and—I believe sincerely—to the inspiration and guidance of God.

Our Bible developed through changing eras of human social evolution, incremental learning, historical dynamics, and scientific development. In ancient times there was very limited understanding of the physical structure of the natural universe because people were limited to what they could see with the eye and what they could imagine.

The discovery of lens and the development of the telescope and microscope did not occur until long after Jesus lived (17th century CE). Reading and writing were not a feature of life for the general populace for many centuries of Hebrew/Israelite/Jewish history. Traditions and genealogies were preserved almost totally by oral passage from father to son in the nomadic and tribal cultures described in the Old Testament. This cultural situation prevailed until after the end of the kingdom period (6th century BCE).

Through the centuries, folklore and superstitions came to be included and carried forward in those oral traditions. I believe that in the great majority of recorded stories there was indeed an actual incident that became the foundation upon which additions and details led to an expanded and often radically changed "story" in generations later.

Keeping in mind the limitations and evolutions noted above, as I address the development of faith, I will not significantly engage in textual criticism—that task belongs to technical scholars and involves problems. *Phases of Faith in the Biblical Story* is intended for people who accept the text as we have it in our Bible.

My purpose is to help readers understand what people through the ages have believed about God and religion, what their religious practices have meant to them, and how they have applied their faith to their lives. I am deeply convinced that God is always active in guiding the human development of religious faith so that in our Bible a stream of truth is preserved that leads humanity upward and prepares us for the awesome life and teachings of Jesus.

A brief statement of textual orientation is appropriate to explain why this writing begins with Genesis 12, instead of Genesis 1. Genesis 1–11 are pre-Hebrew stories. They are insightful parables, similar to ancient primitive origin fables and hero epics. They are not, however, the beginning of the Hebrew story. They did not become part of Jewish religious history until the 6th-5th centuries BCE. The "stream" of Hebrew faith began as a "spring," at the call of Abraham, and "flowed forth" from there.

The "spring" had a time and place. The time was 2000–1900 BCE, and the place was the Near East, Mesopotamia west to the Mediterranean Sea. The culture was tribal, and the climate dry. Some cities existed, but life was largely nomadic herding. Religion was polytheistic, primarily worship of natural objects and forces—sun, moon, air, wind, and water.

Into that world a man named Abram lived, a world-changing religious event happened, and a new kind of religion was born. For that reason, our story begins at Genesis 12:1-3.

The biblical story covers several periods of historical, cultural, and religious development. These divisions are loosely traced through the Old Testament as the patriarchal, tribal, kingdom, and exile periods. Faith development continues in the New Testament with the life and teachings of Jesus and the first centuries of Christianity.

Patriarchal Period

Faith development began with the narrative of a family headed by patriarchs and lasted for about a century and a half (1850–1700 BCE). The lives of the patriarchs (Abraham, Isaac, Jacob, and Joseph) and their wives (Sarah, Rebekah, Leah, Rachel, and Asenath) involved migrations, wanderings, wars, and famines.

The religion of the patriarchs was largely about a call from God, a covenant with God, and the belief in "their" God as a sovereign among other gods worshiped by neighboring tribes. The patriarchal period ended when a famine forced families/people to migrate to Egypt for survival.

Tribal Period

The tribal period includes the story of the twelve sons of Jacob, beginning with their slavery in Egypt and continuing for two and a half centuries (1300–1050 BCE). The leaders through those years were Moses and Aaron, Joshua, tribal family heads, judges, and Samuel (the first leader considered to be a prophet).

Major events included suffering under slavery, Exodus, Sinai, the wilderness, entry into Canaan, settling in tribal areas, and conflict with neighboring Canaanites whom they could not drive out of the land. The primary religious development of the tribal period was the establishment of Mosaic legislation and ritual sacrifice practices.

Kingdom Period

The kingdom period began when the Hebrews/Israelites/Jews insisted on having a king—"like other peoples"—whom they thought could lead them in their battles. Saul, the first king, was tasked with "bringing them together." Then came David, the warrior king, who was victorious in establishing the nation of Israel. Next, Solomon expanded the nation to imperial status, but so burdened the people that the nation divided under Rehoboam after Solomon's death.

The divided kingdoms, Judah and Israel, continued until the Northern Kingdom was destroyed by Assyrian conquest in 722 BCE. Judah continued for more than another century until it fell to Babylonian conquest in 587 BCE, ending the kingdom period that began in 1040 BCE.

Major events of the kingdom period included the coronation of Saul, the building of the Temple, the division into two kingdoms, and the fall of the kingdoms under foreign imperial expansion. The central religious development was the belief that God is enthroned in a palatial city in heaven, patterned after the royal city of Jerusalem built by David and Solomon.

The Exile Period

The period of Babylonian exile and post-exile spanned the remainder of the Old Testament era (587 BCE through the interbiblical centuries). The Exile itself lasted only half a century (587–539 BCE) before the Persian Empire conquered Babylon, and the Persian king Cyrus issued an edict ending the Exile and granting permission for the Jews to return to Judah.

Over a couple of centuries, groups of Jews did return and re-establish Jerusalem and a rebuilt Temple as a struggling "province" under Persian control. That situation continued until the Greek conquest by Alexander the Great in 333 BCE. Greek dominance prevailed until Roman conquest and rule began in 63 BCE. Among the religious events of the exilic/post-exilic period, three are most consequential:

- The recording of oral traditions into written documents that became the Hebrew scriptures and the Christian Old Testament:

Persians required the subject provinces to put local laws into written form to be approved and used in local administrative control. The Jewish people were bereft of being exiled in a foreign land away from their destroyed Temple and Jerusalem. Context convinces me that God inspired the priests and Levites to write the oral traditions to preserve their heritage and the sacred Law of Moses.

- The origin of the synagogue:

Away from the Temple, the Jews' religion could not center in sacrifices and offerings. To preserve the teaching of the Torah, and to provide a center for religious services, the synagogue was established as a place of worship through teaching and prayer. The synagogue became pervasive in Jewish life after the Exile.

- The shared experience and influence upon each other by Judaism and the Persian religion of Zoroastrianism:

After the Exile, post-exilic Judaism was characterized by exclusive monotheism (only one real God) and moral dualism (the existence of an adversary demigod/Satan advocating for evil in the world in competition against God). These beliefs of post-exilic Judaism were carried forward as tenets of faith into the Christian faith.

The biblical story of faith development continues in the New Testament era, beginning with the life and teachings of Jesus (5–4 BCE–c. 30 CE). And in the first centuries after Christ, the disciples of Jesus had to "figure out" what this new faith really meant, how it affected their future lives, and what they could believe about God and life. The story is about the rise of leadership, the spread of the gospel, the development of streams of belief about the nature of Jesus, the character of God, and life in relationship with God.

Different traditions developed that were later put into writing by the Gospel writers, Paul in his letters, and other writers. Together, through three centuries, these came to be considered inspired and sacred and were (in 367 CE) canonized to become our Christian New Testament.

The Christian faith has been, and is, a living faith. It has continued to change through the centuries of church history as the store of human knowledge has grown, as culture has affected it, and as skilled and devoted Christians have searched and applied discovered information and inspired insights. Divine guidance has been an unfailing help in fulfilling humanity's search for light, truth, and abundant life.

...

I readily identify as a non-traditional interpreter of Judeo-Christian tenets of faith. I was trained at the graduate level in systematic theology and ethics, but after forty years of serious study I transitioned into an analytical theologian. Therefore, the explanations and interpretations I will present reflect my developed understanding of religious faith and practice.

As a matter of full disclosure, I understand my role to be "lighting candles" and "planting seeds" of information. I sincerely believe that all persons in reality "create" their own religious faith, responding to the sources of religious teaching and influence they choose to trust. If the subject of this manuscript is of interest to you, and if the information and interpretations presented prove to be helpful to you, I will be grateful for the privilege of having shared your personal journey of faith.

Editor's Note

In the chapters that follow, the author's remarks are divided into two sections:
1. Study / discussion of the biblical text appears in regular font.
2. Contextual background / commentary appears in bold type.

Chapter 1

Religion in the Patriarchal Period

The patriarchal period of Hebrew history begins with Abram/Abraham and continues through the lineage of his son Isaac, Isaac's son Jacob, and Jacob's son Joseph. While seeking to follow God's call to a covenantal religion, they and their wives and children experience migrations, wanderings, wars, and famines—not to mention family conflict. Their story is told in the Old Testament book of Genesis.

Abram/Abraham

Abram ("exalted father") is a native Chaldean, from the city of Ur, a place devoted to the worship of the moon. He grows up in the nomad clan of Terah (11:27-30), migrating from Chaldea to Canaan (11:31). At Haran, 600 miles to the northwest of Ur, they stop and settle. Terah dies there (11:32), but Haran continues to be the home of part of the clan (24:4, 10; 28:2; 29:4-6).

In addition to the Chaldeans' worship of the moon, other cities of Mesopotamia have shrines to various nature deities. This primitive nature worship can hardly be called a religion. It is more akin to respect for and fear of "more than natural forces" that affect "natural objects," which in turn affect the lives of people for either good or bad. Religious practices such as offering sacrifices on altars are believed to influence the deity to favor and bless instead of to disfavor and chastise the tribal groups over which the deity reigns.

The dominant feature of Haran is the massive Arabian desert. Lying over and around the desert is a fertile crescent, made up of the Mesopotamian valley on the east, the Syrian mountain range across the northern top, and the Lebanon-Canaan "land bridge" on the west along the eastern shore of the Mediterranean Sea.

Caravans, armies, and migrating people do not cross the desert. They follow the fertile crescent. Trade routes, military movements, and migrations follow that route from Babylon/Persia, to Assyria/Syria, to Canaan, to Egypt in the Old Testament records.

The migration of the Terah clan is not an unusual action. Herdsmen in those areas are forced to be nomadic because the semi-arid climate makes vegetation and grazing scarce. Frequent droughts often force major migrations. There is no information in the text (11:31) about the motivation for Terah/Abram's migration to Haran.

Call and Response

At Haran, Abram experiences a personal command from God: "Go from your country … to the land that I will show you" (12:1). This is a new thing in the history of religions. It is described as a personal contact from a deity to a human. The text does not describe what Abram believes about the nature and character of the God who is commanding him, but does inform us about God. The speaker is identified as "the Lord," *YeHVaH* (Jehovah) in Hebrew. The call of Abram is the historic beginning of a revealed religion.

The call of Abraham as a new thing in religion reflects the difference between "revealed" religion and "discovery" religion.

Nature religions, animistic religions, and moral character religions originate and develop when people try to determine what influences life, and how life turns out best. A person, or persons, then create religious practices such as building shrines and altars in attempts to influence such forces or spirits for good. Then arises the following of a leader who has discovered something supernatural, and a religious system becomes established.

Discovery religions originate and develop by people searching upward. By contrast, revealed religion begins with God reaching down to make himself and his will for people known.

Judaism, Christianity, and Islam are the three major historic religions that identify as revealed religions. These three are founded on belief in revelation from God. They differ, however, in what is believed to have been revealed by God about God's character and God's requirements for humankind.

The text does not record any questioning and deliberating by Abram as part of his experiencing and responding to such a life-changing instruction. He is already a man of mature, even advanced, age (12:4). He has lived in a moon-worshipping culture all those years. Even so, surely questions remain: "Who is this God who is commanding me? What else will be required of me if I make this migration? What is this about 'all the families of the earth'?"

In a tribal culture where clans and cities build shrines to and worship multiple deities, it seems certain that God's personal "breaking into" Abram's life with a command and offer of covenant relationship is an awesome experience for Abram. All we have in the record is his obedient response: "So Abram went, as the Lord had told him" (12:4).

Life in Canaan

The migration of Abram's family covers another 400 miles, southwest from Haran, to Shechem in central Canaan. Imagine the time it takes them to cover the distance of a thousand miles, with grazing flocks and herds, from Ur to Haran to Shechem. A major part of their lives, and major changes in history and religion, are covered in nine verses of biblical text.

When the group arrives in Canaan, a land already populated by Canaanite tribes, Abram senses that God is affirming to him that this is the land to which God is leading him. This is to be a "homeland" for them (12:7). Abram, in turn, builds an altar there, and we can assume he offers sacrifices of the sort he believes are appropriate. He seems to be affirming his acceptance of God as sovereign, the reality of covenant as the basis of his clan's relationship with God, and the land as God's gift to them. A tenet of religious faith is beginning to be revealed.

Religious faith in Abram's time is based on the belief that gods are striving to gain possessive control over more lands and people. The sovereignty of a deity is determined by how powerful the deity is compared to others. In doing so, the most powerful can effectively rule over more land and people, and can even eliminate an entire population through ethnic cleansing. This is the religious faith issue involved in Abram's faith. Abram believes that the God who is calling him to covenant is able to make Canaan "God's land" and give it to Abram's descendants as people "chosen" to be "God's people." That faith manifests itself in Hebrew/Israelite/Jewish religion from Abram onward.

Later, belief in one God as universally sovereign leads many (or most) non-Jews generally to believe that exclusive divine promises to the Jews as recorded in the Old Testament are not applicable. As monotheistic religions develop, belief in one God with universal sovereignty replaces belief in polytheism and localized sovereignty by deities. From the perspective of monotheistic religion, it seems surely that the concept of "chosen people's promised land" was never a divine intention. We will, nevertheless, meet that belief and will need to understand its basis as we study religion in the Old Testament.

...

Prior to the introduction of "covenant" between God and Abraham, the relationship between deity and people has been unilateral. Nature religions believe in supernatural forces, not personal spirits. The "force" functions, and humans receive the consequences. People offer sacrifices and hope for favorable effects. God offers Abram a bilateral, personal relationship in the establishment of covenant. Each party will invest something into the relationship. Each will, in turn, receive something from the relationship.

Abram and his clan consider themselves established in a homeland, given to them by divine action. They move about the area as nomad shepherds. They are as a group few enough that they represent no great threat to the Canaanite tribes. The Canaanites generally tolerate the clan, although there are occasional conflicts when they compete for the same areas for grazing or wells and other water sources (13:1-7, 21:25-32). Despite their toleration by the natives, Abram and his people are considered foreigners.

Abram is called "the Hebrew," in contrast to the kings who are identified with the local tribes (14:1-9). The name "Hebrew" is derived from a root word meaning "from beyond the river." Abram is branded as "the foreigner who came from beyond the river," a reference that becomes an identifying name.

Abram is from Chaldea, a land beyond the Euphrates, the river being referred to here. The Euphrates River is considered a dividing line between major geographical areas when referred to from both directions. This original difference about "whose land this is" becomes a tenet of faith for Hebrews, and has continued through the centuries as a cause of conflict between Jews and non-Jews.

Family Deception and Jealousy

Abram's early family story (12:10-20) reflects how cultural practices and religious beliefs are interwoven. When a famine leads the clan to go to Egypt, Abram fears for his life, thinking some Egyptian might kill him to get possession of Sarai. So, Abram instructs his wife Sarai to claim she is his sister. As a result, she is taken into Pharaoh's house and Abram is treated well. "The Lord afflicts Pharaoh," however, because of Sarai and the deception is exposed. Pharaoh challenges Abram for what he has done, returns Sarai to Abram, and sends the clan out of Egypt (12:10-20).

The Abram-Sarai-Pharaoh story reveals two cultural practices of the patriarchal period. First, women are treated as possessions of men, to be used in ways most beneficial to men. Kings "gathered unto themselves" groups of women (harems), competing to see who has the largest harem as a sign of status. Treatment of Sarai, good or bad, is for Abram's benefit, not Sarai's. Second, a religious belief is reflected in that both Abram and Pharaoh believe that Abram's God disapproves of Sarai being placed in the ruler's house, and therefore God afflicts Pharaoh's house as chastisement until Sarai is returned.

In the primitive age of the patriarchs and until after the Babylonian captivity (6th c. BCE), all the varied forms of religion that develop believe in "moral monism," or that both good and bad have the same source. However, if their God/god is pleased with them, they will receive favor and blessing. If their God/god is displeased with them, disfavor and punishment will come upon them. The two key factors that determine the pleasure or displeasure, favor or disfavor, of their God/god is whether they are exclusively loyal to the deity to whom they "belong," and whether they are obedient in following all the commands of their God/god. In the incident about Sarai and Pharaoh, their faith leads them to believe that Abram's God is taking Abram's side, chastising the Pharaoh for what he is doing, and the Egyptian gods can do nothing on the Pharaoh's behalf to prevent it.

In addition to deception within the nuclear family, jealousy within the clan is brewing. The herds become so large that scarcity of grazing leads to family members' separating to dwell in different areas (13:2-7). Lot chooses the Jordan valley in Sodom, while Abram settles on the *negeb* (desert) near Hebron (13:8-12). Lot's move to Sodom, where the men are described as wicked (13:13), begins a story to be continued later.

Jealousy also develops within Abram's household. After Abram and Lot separate, the Lord appears to Abram and promises to give him and his offspring all the land of Canaan (13:14-15). Abram has no offspring, however, as Sarai is childless (11:30, 16:1).

In his culture, a son is considered vital for the continuation of the family line and heritage. Following accepted cultural practice, Sarai has Abram beget a child with her servant maid Hagar (16:3-4). But Hagar then becomes "proud," and Sarai becomes jealous. Sarai "deals harshly" with Hagar, so the servant flees into the wilderness but later returns. Her son Ishmael is born into Abram's household (16:15).

Renewal of the Covenant

Several years later God renews the covenant with Abram, promising to make Abram "the father of many nations" and changing Abram's name to Abraham (17:4-5). As "a sign of the covenant" (17:11), circumcision is introduced. Beginning with Abraham and Ishmael, circumcision becomes a ritual required of all Hebrew men and boys.

God also changes Sarai's name to Sarah and promises that Sarah will bear them a son (17:16-19). An item of religious faith is described here: Sarah's childlessness, and promised motherhood, is believed to be by choice and an act of God (16:2, 17:19).

Several covenant renewals are recorded in Genesis, including the beginning of the practice of circumcision among the Hebrews (17:10-11, 23-27). This practice includes two meanings: It provides tribal and religious identification to differentiate Hebrews from non-Hebrews, and "to set apart" those who are included in the "covenant people" from those who are not. It is also a covenant-sealing ritual. The Hebrew word meaning "to make a covenant" comes from the root *BaRaTh*, or "to cut" (as "to cut a covenant"). To fulfill the ritual of sealing a covenant with blood, in both Hebrew culture and religion, circumcision provides a "blood sacrifice" as a covenant seal.

As confirmation of God's promise that Sarah will bear a son, the Lord appears to Abraham (Gen 18:1) in a theophany (defined as "a visible manifestation by a deity to a human person, or group of persons"). Three men visit Abraham, who shows obeisance and hospitality to them (18:2-8). The visitors inform Abraham that Sarah will bear a son. The promise is incredible to both because of their advanced ages.

Sodom and Lot

As Abraham's "visitors" are leaving, God "tells" Abraham about the fate of Sodom (18:17-21). Abraham then intercedes for the "righteous" who may be there, including his nephew Lot (18:22-33).

At Sodom the visitors are met by Lot and persuaded to come into his home. Trouble arises, however. The men of Sodom gather, insisting to know "who it is" that Lot has welcomed into "their town" and into his home (19:5). They reveal their own distrust of Lot as a foreigner who has settled among them and would now even judge them (19:9). The visitors rescue Lot, shut the door, and "blind" the men of Sodom into confusion until they go away (19:10-11). Their mob intentions are thwarted.

In the continuing story, the messengers instruct Lot and all his kin to leave Sodom immediately. All of the family members flee, except Lot's wife, to nearby Zoar as Sodom and the Siddim Valley are destroyed by fire.

The story of "Sodom's evil" becomes in Hebrew history a record of both moral evil and racial prejudice. The demand "that we may know them" (19:5) and the description of Lot's daughters "who have not known a man" (v. 8) live in tradition as referring to sexual intercourse as abuse and moral evil (homosexual in v. 5, heterosexual in v. 8). Lot's response reflects that he considers his hospitality responsibility to be more important than protecting his daughters from such horrid abuse. The response of the people of Sodom reflects their prejudice against "outsiders" in their city, just as the Canaanites had felt resentment toward the foreigner Abraham and his family. Verse 9 has the character of a sneer included in it, as "this fellow…an alien."

The Sodom story has been used as a basis for declaring sodomy (homosexual sex) sinful. This passage does not support that interpretation, although other Old Testament texts do prohibit male copulation and bestiality (Lev. 18:22-23, 20:13-16). The basis for the Sodom incident being understood as involving homosexual conduct comes from the demand, "Bring them out to us, so that we may 'know' them" (v. 5). This is to understand the word "know" as in Genesis 4:1, "Now the man 'knew' Eve his wife, and she conceived…" The Hebrew word in both texts comes from the root *YaDa*, meaning "to see, gain knowledge, become acquainted." The word was widely used and had derived meanings such as to know intimately enough to have sexual intercourse and to refer to crimes against nature. The context in the Sodom passage refers to a question about identification: "Who are these strangers?"

Use of the words "men" and "angels" also needs explanation. The Hebrew word *eNaSh* is a basic term for "man." It occurs in Genesis 18:2, 16 and 19:4-10 to refer to the three "visitors." It is the same word used to refer to the "men of Sodom" in 19:4-10. The Hebrew word *MaLaKh* means "a messenger, a person sent on a task or with a message" representing "an individual, a king, or God." It occurs in Genesis 19:1, 15 and is translated "angels." The word angel is not a translation from Hebrew, but derives from the Greek word aggelos, "a messenger," the same as Hebrew *MaLaKh*. When the Old Testament was translated from Hebrew into Greek, "angel" was used to translate *MaLaKh* when the "messenger" was understood to be a representative of God. There is no reason indicated for different words being used to refer to the "visitors."

Genesis 19 concludes with the record of incest between Lot's daughters and their father. The daughters are concerned about keeping their tribal lineage exclusive. They believe that Sodom's destruction is so widespread that no appropriate kin will survive to become fathers of children for them (19:31), so they devise a plan to beget children with their father (19:32-36): They get him drunk and sleep with their father, resulting in pregnancies that lead to the birth of two sons: Moab and Ammon. Lot is not "heard from" again except in tradition.

The record of incest between Lot and his daughters is not described as evil in Genesis 19, but incest is prohibited as evil in Mosaic law (Lev. 18:8-10, 20:11-12)—although marriage with close cousins would be allowed to avoid intermarriage with Canaanites (24:1-4).

The Lot story is informative from two points of view. The daughters' plan to have children with their father included getting him so drunk that he would not be conscious of the acts. If looked at from the point of view of the "children" of Lot's daughters, the parentage reflects well on their heritage. The sons resulting from the incest are described as the ancestral origins of the Moabites and the Ammonites. Although non-Israelite, because of their lineage, these tribes could potentially claim "patriarchal" heritage, back to Haran and Terah (11:31).

However, in the Hebrew/Israelite religious faith the "chosen line" of "chosen people" as established by divine "promise" to Abraham would prevent this. Only direct descendants of Abraham would carry forth the line of heritage: essentially, other people would be dismissed.

Isaac

When Abraham is 100 years old, his son of promise is born. The birth of Isaac causes the family dynamics of competition and jealousy between the two mothers, Sarah and Hagar, to fester and finally erupt. Sarah will not tolerate Ishmael having anything to do with Isaac, not even play with him (21:8-9). She insists that Hagar and Ishmael be banished from the family (21:10). In the wilderness, God provides for the two and also assures Abraham that his first son will have a noble future (21:13, 18-20).

At the time of the expulsion, Ishmael appears to be still dependent on the mother for care and provision (21:14-19). Isaac is described as having just been weaned (21:8). In the previous record of the circumcision of Abraham and Ishmael, the boy is said to be thirteen years old (17:25). That is the same time difference as in Abraham's age at the two births (16:16, 17:1). The descriptions of Ishmael in the story are likely a matter of editorial arrangement when the oral traditions were later put into writing. The central focus is on the establishment of a "line of promise," believed to be determined by divine choice generation by generation.

Sometime after Ishmael leaves Abraham's household, God tests Abraham's loyalty and faithfulness by commanding him to take Isaac to Moriah and once there to "slay and burn" Isaac. Abraham "hears" God and prepares to do just that. On the mountain, with Isaac bound on the altar, and Abraham with knife raised, only then does Abraham "hear" God say, "Do not lay your hand on the boy…" (22:12). God then supplies a ram for the sacrifice and confirms his blessing on Abraham.

In the sacrifice of Isaac, does God change his mind at the last moment? Is it really a test to see how far Abraham will go? What does this reveal about Abraham's religious faith? Context is vital for understanding this momentous story. The context involves the state of religious faith in primitive times and the interrelated influence of tribal culture and polytheistic religion. This faith/religion included human sacrifice as a way to express devotion to one's deity, whether God or an idol.

Abraham certainly goes to Moriah with the clear intention to slay and burn his son. What is Abraham "believing" that makes it even possible that he can "hear" God commanding him to sacrifice Isaac? Is he haunted by the idea that pagans can be more devoted to their gods than he is? Does the "test" really arise out of Abraham's developing faith?

The answer is reflected in the climax of the story. When Abraham raises the knife to make the sacrifice to prove his devotion, God who has called him to covenant overwhelms him with the conviction that "the God he worships" does not even countenance such sacrifice. The prohibition of human sacrifice is established as a religious tenet of faith that prevails thereafter in Hebrew religion (Deut. 12:19-31, 18:9-10).

Another developing religious belief is also reflected in this story. The earliest belief about death was that the soul is only the "animating" feature of the body, the breath of life that dies with the body (3:19, see Jas. 4:14). Belief in *Sheol*, the place of the dead, was long believed to be an "end" to which the "soul" goes at physical death, to a shadowy existence to fade away, and from which to never return (Job 7:9, 21).

As religious beliefs developed through the centuries about the soul and death, people began to believe in the integrity of the soul and hope beyond death. The psalmist sings, "If I make my bed in *Sheol*, you (God) are there" (Ps. 139:8). Hannah sings of the Lord who "kills and brings to life," who "brings down to *Sheol* and raises up" (1 Sam. 2:6). Ecclesiastes records the belief that when the "silver cord is snapped," the "dust returns to the earth as it was, and the breath returns to God who gave it" (12:6-7). And Isaiah writes that in God's new age, "Your dead shall live, their corpses shall rise. O dwellers in the dust, awake and sing for joy" (Isa. 26:19).

As Abraham and Isaac leave the servants and go toward the mountain for Isaac's death, Abraham says to the young men, "... the boy and I will go over there; we will worship, and then we will come back to you" (22:5). That "man of faith" who so trusts and is so devoted to God that he is willing to sacrifice his son, also believes that God is able to make things right even if it means raising the dead to life. Abraham stands as a mountain peak in that great developing stream of faith.

A third item of faith is prominently important in this passage and throughout the Bible. It is the matter of how God communicates with human persons. The text reads that God "said" things to Abraham. God is spirit. God was fully God before anything material existed. God has no physical body. God does not speak as humans speak. God does not speak to the ear; God speaks to the heart. In biblical times, sometimes God's message comes by a messenger and other times in a dream. And, I am persuaded that God also inspires an awareness/calling/truth/command directly into the heart/soul of a person.

For accurate Bible study, it is important to remember that the message spoken or written is only as correct as the messenger is rightly informed and reliable. The religious beliefs reflected in the full span of biblical documents are often accurate and meaningful to the time and context of the people and events, but not to tenets of faith revealed and/or arrived at and believed in later eras.

After the death of Sarah, Abraham sends his servant to Haran to secure a wife for Isaac. The servant meets Rebekah, a cousin, and concludes she is the chosen one (24:15, 25:20). The servant is eager to return to Isaac with her. Although her culture calls for men to make decisions, and wives and daughters to obey, Rebekah's family lets her make the decision (24:51, 54-59). She chooses to leave and then becomes the wife of Isaac.

After Abraham's death, Isaac becomes the patriarch of the clan. His story then revolves around his family. Rebekah has a difficult pregnancy, and receives a message from God that she will bear twins and the elder will serve the younger (25:22-23). The younger twin, Jacob, is born holding the heel of the elder twin, Esau (25:26). (The name Jacob is derived from a root meaning "heel grabber" or one who trips up another and takes over the lead.)

The "line of promise" succession belief plays a prominent role in Isaac's family. Isaac loves Esau (25:28), and expects him to be heir of the clan head after him (27:4). The "clan blessing" is believed to be the divine bestowal of "line of promise" status (27:27-29). Rebekah loves Jacob (25:28), and schemes with him to gain the clan blessing on his behalf.

Jacob, the supplanter, cons Esau out of his elder-son birthright (25:27-34). Rebekah schemes with Jacob to steal near-blind Isaac's clan blessing for Jacob (27:5-30). The parents differ about the validity of "divine establishment" of the first-born heritage, with the family dynamics appearing to be "wife wins over husband." Belief develops that bestowal of the "line of promise" blessing on Jacob comes by divine leading (25:23), a thread that follows in Jacob's story. Isaac is reduced to a supporting role until his death (35:27-29).

The offer of Isaac as a sacrifice is the first of a series of events marking a major transition in Hebrew history, as follows: the sacrifice (22:1-14), a renewed affirmation of covenant promises to Abraham (22:15-19), the dismissal of the remainder of the Terah clan (22:20-24), the death of Sarah (23:1-20), the marriage of Isaac (24:1-67), the death of Abraham (25:1-11), and the dismissal of Ishmael (25:12-18). This appears to be a clear indication of editorial planning by the scribes who wrote the oral traditions into documents during and after the Babylonian Exile.

Jacob

Rebekah's leadership in her family continues when she persuades Isaac to send Jacob to Haran to seek a wife (27:41–28:5). At Bethel, Jacob has a vision of God affirming the clan blessing to him (28:10-17). In Haran, Jacob becomes established in Laban's family. He loves Rachel, but is deceived by Laban into marrying both Leah and Rachel (29:16-30).

Jacob's family grows: Leah and her maid bear eight sons and a daughter for Jacob. Rachel's maid bears two sons and Rachel gives birth to one son, Joseph, while they are living in Haran (29:31–30:24). Jacob becomes wealthy managing Laban's flocks and herds. He seems to prosper by his knowledge of animal breeding and herd manipulation, but Laban's sons believe Jacob is stealing from their father. The underlying Hebrew religious belief is that his prosperity is the result of divine blessing (30:27-43).

Jealousy and conflict develop within Jacob's family, and between Jacob and Laban. Jacob decides it is wise to leave Haran and return home to Canaan. His wives agree that they have no heritage in Haran, so they plan to leave while Laban is away. Rachel steals the

Religion in the Patriarchial Period

family "household gods" (31:1-21). They depart, but after three days Laban learns of the theft and secret departure and chases after Jacob's group.

Laban is distressed about losing his gods, and searches the family's tents for them. Rachel sits on them and claims to be ritually unclean so she cannot stand. She tricks her father and keeps the *teraphim*. Ironically, Laban believes that the absence of his gods will be a great loss. Rachel and Jacob believe the pagan gods are helpless before Jacob's God. They do not fear to scorn Laban's gods by having Rachel sit on them, even though she is "unclean" (31:19-35). Finally, Jacob and Laban part as friends and agree on a boundary across which they will not cross to rob each other (31:22-55).

Before entering Canaan, Jacob must meet Esau. He fears that Esau's wrath has not abated, following the loss of his birthright, and his vow of vengeance will be violent. Jacob sends an envoy to ask for peace, and Esau comes to meet him with four hundred men (32:3-6). Jacob tries to "buy him off" with gifts he sends on ahead (32:7-21).

Jacob then takes his family across the Jabbok River (32:22-23). Through the night a "man" wrestles with Jacob, but cannot prevail against him (32:24). At dawn the man asks for release. Jacob asks for a blessing. The man asks Jacob his name, and Jacob replies. The man says, "Your name is Jacob no longer. Your name is now Israel." Jacob/Israel is blessed but left lame, and the man is heard from no more (32:24-32). Jacob names the place Peniel.

When meeting Esau is imminent, Jacob arranges his family: maids and their children first, Leah and her children next, then Rachel and Joseph last. Jacob goes before them. Esau greets him with a warm embrace and asks about his family (33:1-7). They haggle about the proffered gift of cattle. Esau accepts (33:8-11) and then proposes they travel together, with him leading. Jacob declines "on behalf of" his children and flocks. Esau offers to leave some of his men with Jacob's party, but Jacob again declines (33:12-17). They obviously don't trust each other. They make alternate proposals, each seeking to protect himself from the other.

Jacob settles for a period at Shechem among a Hivite tribe. Trouble arises about intermarriage. Both sides practice deception, and violent vengeance results. Jacob hears God calling for repentant cleansing of pagan practices, and for a renewal of covenant at Bethel (34:1–35:15).

From Bethel, Jacob's clan continues to move southward. Rachel is pregnant. Near Bethlehem she gives birth to Benjamin and then dies. Jacob's group goes on to Hebron to Isaac's home and settles there. Isaac dies and is buried by Esau and Jacob (35:16-29).

The remainder of Jacob's life is the story of Joseph's rise to prominence (37:1-2) and the migration of the clan to Egypt during a famine. Jacob dies in Egypt and is embalmed. His sons take his body to Canaan and bury it in the cave at Macpelah (50:13).

The beliefs reflected in the stories of Jacob's life are a continuation of those that have developed in the clan, based on God's covenant with Abraham. The clan believes in a line of promise established by God, though Isaac and Rebekah differ about which of the sons is destined to carry forth that line. The developing tradition that Jacob is the chosen one is established by his experience of covenant renewal at Bethel as he flees toward Haran (28:13-15).

In Haran, culture leads to Laban's deception and Jacob's marriage to Leah before Rachel, elder before younger. The effect of cultural practice is overcome, however, through Jacob's love of Rachel and the birth of Joseph who will be the "line of promise" carrier in the next generation.

An interesting bit about both culture and religion is reflected in the story of the Jacob family leaving Haran. When Jacob tells Rachel and Leah that God is instructing him to leave and go to Canaan, they agree to the move. As women, they will inherit nothing of their father's estate. They have been "sold in marriage" and treated as foreigners (31:13-16). Rachel attempts to gain something by stealing the household gods (*teraphim*), graven images made in human form to represent a deity being "worshipped" by a family. The images are believed to be powerful enough that whoever possesses them is dominant in the life of the family. Laban's gods are small enough that Rachel can hide them in her camel saddle.

Jacob's experience at Peniel (32:24-32) reflects a significant religious belief. The story is told as a theophany, with the "man" representing God. The name change reveals the meaning of this experience. Recall the meaning of the name Jacob, "heel-grabber," one who grabs another's heel in the race to trip up and take the lead, to supplant (25:26). Jacob has lived all his life as a supplanter—deceiving, outwitting, stealing, manipulating.

The dynamic involved in the name change seems to indicate that the man Jacob wrestles with is his own guilty self, the Spirit of God doing the work of convicting. Jacob is facing a meeting with Esau the day after the restless night. He knows not if Esau is still determined to kill him. God deals with him in a way he has not known before.

The name change describes this experience as a personal conversion. No longer is he to be Jacob, a scheming supplanter. He is to be Israel, one who has met God "face to face" (the meaning of Peniel). He is not destroyed, as it is believed to be the fate of anyone who does see God. This is a unique experience of belief at this historic time. God is believed to relate to people as a covenant group. All are in God's favor, or all are subject to chastisement. Jacob is personally convicted of guilt and named a new man.

Joseph

Rachel's firstborn son is Jacob's favorite. Jealousy, trouble, and conflict result. Joseph's story is filled with human dynamics and religious faith. Jacob's favoritism is clearly obvious. He keeps Joseph around home with him and dresses him in fancy clothes (37:3), while Joseph's brothers live on the move as nomad shepherds. Joseph has two dreams that cast him as superior to the others, and he appears to delight in telling the family of his dreams (37:5-11).

Jacob sends Joseph to find the flocks and see if things are going well. The brothers conspire to kill Joseph, but Reuben saves his life and intends to send him back home. The other brothers choose instead to sell him to traders in a Midianite caravan. The brothers strip Joseph of his coat, soak it in blood, and send it to their father, who knows it is Joseph's. In his mind, he is certain a wild beast has killed his son (Gen 37:12-34).

Joseph is taken to Egypt and sold to Potiphar, a military officer, as a slave. Potiphar prospers with Joseph as his house manager and entrusts his entire management to Joseph (39:1-6). Potiphar's wife is infatuated with the handsome Joseph and propositions him, but Joseph refuses. She then grabs his cloak as he flees, and subsequently accuses him of insult and assault to Potiphar and Joseph is thrown into prison (39:7-21).

In each of the episodes the Lord is with Joseph and causes his integrity to gain favorable treatment. In prison the keeper is impressed with Joseph and puts the prisoners in his charge. Two of the king's servants who are in the prison have dreams and tell them to Joseph. He interprets their dreams, which come true as Joseph has envisioned them. The butler is released, and the baker is executed (40:5-23). Joseph has asked the butler to tell his story to the king, but the butler fails to do so (40:14, 23).

Pharaoh has a dream that puzzles his dream interpreters. The butler then remembers Joseph's request. Joseph hears and interprets Pharaoh's dreams about seven years of bountiful harvests, followed by seven years of famine (41:1-32). Joseph tells Pharaoh to store reserves during the years of bounty for the coming years of famine. Pharaoh approves the plan, assigns the task to Joseph, and makes him manager of the nation—second only to Pharaoh himself (41:33-45).

Famine also comes in Canaan, where Joseph's family lives. Jacob sends Joseph's brothers, without Benjamin, to Egypt to buy grain. Joseph recognizes his brothers, but they do not recognize him (42:1-8). Testing and contesting follow. Joseph insists they send one brother for Benjamin while the rest stay in prison, to prove they are honest and not spies. Joseph decides instead to "hold" Simeon as security and to free the other brothers. He "sells" them grain, but has their money hidden back in the sacks (42:9-28).

The brothers return home. They have grain and "their" money, but Simeon is left in prison. They tell Jacob about their time in Egypt and the requirement that Benjamin return with them if they wish to purchase grain. Jacob has a serious dilemma: Joseph and Simeon are gone, and Benjamin must go if grain is to be purchased again (42:29-38).

The grain supply runs dangerously low while the famine continues. The need for food becomes severe enough that Jacob is forced to let Benjamin go to Egypt, but Jacob also sends some gifts and "double" the money. In Egypt, Joseph treats his brothers well, dines with them, and learns about the family. But the brothers still do not recognize him. He again has their money hidden in their sacks, and in Benjamin's sack is Joseph's personal silver cup (43:1–44:3).

Joseph sends after them to "find" his cup and bring them back. Joseph tests his brothers severely, declaring that Benjamin must "pay the penalty" for the "crime." Judah pleads for Benjamin and offers to "bear the guilt" himself, lest the loss of Benjamin cost their father his life (44:4-34). Joseph has had enough, so he identifies himself and the brothers are reconciled (45:1-15).

Pharaoh invites Joseph to bring his family to Egypt to dwell. Jacob rejoices to know Joseph is alive, and agrees for the clan to go to Egypt, but leaves with a sense of promise that God will accompany them to Egypt and bring them again to Canaan. The records of the Hebrew patriarchal period end. The story of the "sons of Jacob" and the bondage of their families begins (46:1-7).

Note

[1] Samuel E. Balentine, *The Torah's Vision of Worship*, (Minneapolis: Fortress Press, 1999), 50-51. Minneapolis: Fortress Press, 1999), 50-51.

Chapter 2
Religion in the Tribal Period

The Patriarchal period of Hebrew history ended when a famine in Canaan forced Jacob's family to migrate to Egypt to receive Joseph's care. In Egypt, the tribal culture and the covenant religion of Abraham continue to be the religious practice among the Hebrews without major change. The Egypt era sets the stage for an essentially new beginning under the leadership of Moses. Whereas only a nomad clan went to Egypt, a large mass of people came out.

Abraham and his family of nomadic herders did not present a significant threat to the native Canaanite inhabitants: they were tolerated as "foreigners" without serious conflict. Much later, the invading army led by Joshua presents a different situation entirely. Joshua and the Israelites come believing their God had given the land to their ancestors, and that they are under orders to possess the land by either driving out all the inhabiting tribes or annihilating them. Generations of war are inevitable.

The Exodus, the Sinai time of organization, and the development of Mosaic law and practices are historic events that describe the "new beginning" of the Israelite heritage of "chosen people" in a "promised land."

Joseph's Last Years

The Hebrew clan of Jacob arrives in Egypt in the land of Goshen, and a family reunion is held (Gen. 46:26-30). Joseph takes charge and tells his family to identify as shepherds, because he has a plan (Gen. 47:1-6). He knows that Egyptians detest shepherds, for they are farmers on irrigated fields along the Nile. The family members go to Pharaoh, identified as shepherds, and ask to be permitted to live in Goshen, in the northeast corner of Egypt. A part of the Nile River delta, Goshen has rich alluvial soil and is well-watered. And, it is near Canaan—with homeland ties for the Hebrew hearts. Pharaoh approves the request, and Joseph has accomplished his purpose.

When Jacob is near death, he passes on the "clan blessing" to one of Joseph's sons. In the blessing Jacob crosses his hands and blesses Ephraim, the younger, instead of Manasseh. Jacob also asks Joseph to take his body back to Canaan for burial (Gen. 47:27-31).

> The religious beliefs reflected in the migration and settlement to Egypt is a continuation of the features of the covenant with Abraham. God is still believed to be especially identified with Canaan. Jacob agrees to go to Egypt after he hears God promise to watch over his family and bring them back to their promised homeland (Gen. 46:3-4). Joseph continues to carry forward that promise (Gen. 50:24).

> The "son of promise" and the "line of promise" are believed to be of divine design—that God reveals the carrier of the line by divine choice in each generation. Whereas in the clan culture priority status is given to the firstborn son, in the line of promise the son is believed to be chosen by divine selection.
>
> In addition, belief in divine design means that God controls the events of every day and the fate of individuals. Joseph reflects this belief in the way he deals with his brothers. They fear Joseph will avenge "… all the wrong we did to him." Joseph, in turn, shows kindness and forgives them. He declares it has all happened by divine design to send him to Egypt to prepare for the preservation of the clan in the great famine (Gen. 50:15-21).

Joseph lives to see his great-grandchildren born (Gen. 50:23), but the time comes when Joseph's influence is past and forgotten. Life changes for the Israelites.

The Early Life of Moses

The Egyptians come to fear the Israelites as aliens, who might become military enemies in war. They try to subdue them with burdens and reduce them to slavery (Exod. 1:7-14). The Egyptians attempt to kill all newborn boys since they could pose a future threat: Girls make good servants, but boys can become rebel soldiers (Exod. 1:15-22).

Under such peril a son is born to a Levite family, but his birth is hidden. His mother plans to save his life by placing him in a basket where an Egyptian princess will find him (Exod. 2:1-6). His sister watches and suggests their mother to the princess as a wet nurse. The princess adopts him, names him Moses, and places him with his own mother to care for until he is weaned (Exod. 2:4-10). Moses then grows up in Pharaoh's court.

But Moses does not become an Egyptian (Exod. 2:11). His Hebrew heritage, apparently taught him by his mother, is "who he knew himself to be." His identity expresses itself when he sees injustice and cruelty imposed on Israelites. When he reacts and kills an Egyptian, and Pharaoh learns about it, Moses has to flee for his life (Exod. 2:14b-15).

Moses leaves Egypt and goes southeast, as a young man alone in the wilderness, into the land of Midian. There he becomes a shepherd, marries Zipporah, and becomes the father of a son, Gershom (Exod. 2:21-22). The stage is set for a major religious event.

The Preparation of Moses for Leadership

As Moses is tending his father-in-law's sheep on a mountain called Horeb/Sinai, he is encountered by God (Exod. 3:1-10). A burning bush captures his attention. As he approaches the bush, he hears God tell him, "This is holy ground." God brings to his memory the suffering of the Israelites and reminds Moses that God has "seen it all" and is ready to act to redeem his people.

Moses is astounded when he hears God telling him that he, Moses, is to go back to Egypt and lead the Israelites out of bondage and back home to Canaan (Exod. 3:10). Moses protests, "Why me, Lord?" and gives reasons for "Why not!" (Exod. 3:11; 4:1, 10). God removes these "excuses" one by one. Moses then asks one crucial question: "If I go, who shall I say sent me?" If I say, "The God of your fathers," and they ask, "What is his name?" What shall I say to them?

God answers, "Tell them my name is *YaHWeH*,...tell them *I AM* has sent me to you" (Exod. 3:14). Moses then hears God give him instructions about what to say to the Israelites, making promises of deliverance to them.

This experience of Moses is similar to the Haran call to Abraham (Gen. 12:1-3), in which God met him and set him into a role of leadership. This is a "divinely revealed" religious experience (Exod. 3:2-4), not "humanly fashioned" on the basis of search and discovery.

Two matters of religious significance are reflected in this exchange between God and Moses: the nature of God and the way God communicates with people.

First, the nature of God is revealed in the divine name I AM. Biblical religion is founded on God as the origin and creator of all physical matter and the giver of all life. This means that God was fully God as pure spirit before any form of matter existed. The name I AM in first-person present tense means "Self-Existing One, Non-Created One." And the concept "God" means "The Supreme Being," which is a superlative, exclusive nature of deity. Such a monotheistic tenet of faith was not established early in the Israelite faith, but is clearly present in the divine name.

Throughout the Bible, God is described as "speaking." This is problematic since God, by nature, is pure Spirit. Our difficulty in describing communication lies in the limitation of our human language. Psalm 19:3-4 affirms that in the heavens and in nature "there is no speech, nor are there words...yet their voice (message) goes out through all the earth." God does not speak to the ear; God speaks to the heart. For Moses, the "burning bush" catches his attention, but the "voice" he hears changes his life. Numberless others through the ages have "heard," as did Moses.

The situation is ready for Moses to return to Egypt, gain the trust of his Israelite kin, and begin a contest with the Pharaoh to "deliver" the people from bondage.

The Contest in Egypt and the Exodus

After Aaron meets Moses and joins him in leadership, together they convince the Israelite leadership that God is, in fact, acting to secure their deliverance (Exod. 4:27-31). They first ask Pharaoh for permission to go three days into the wilderness for a festival time with their God. Pharaoh refuses, and orders their workloads to be increased (Exod. 5:1-9). After a series of plagues, Pharaoh grants them release to go out of the land (Exod. 6:1-12:36).

The last plague is the death of all firstborn Egyptians, both people and cattle (Exod. 11:5). The Israelites are spared in the plague by the Passover, an event involving sacrifice, meal, and marking. God instructs that a lamb is to be slaughtered and its blood spread on the doorposts and lintels of the Israelites' homes (Exod. 12:7). The meat will then be roasted and eaten with unleavened bread and bitter herbs (Exod. 12:8-10). They are to spend the night and eat the Passover meal, but be dressed and ready to leave their homes (Exod. 12:11).

The death plague devastates the Egyptians. First, they drive the Israelites out (Exod. 12:33), but then, realizing what they have done, send the army to stop them (Exod. 14:5-9). The Israelites are camped by the sea, but Moses persuades them to start moving (Exod. 14:10-18).

A cloudy darkness settles behind the Israelites and stops the Egyptian army. Through the night an east wind blows the tide and bares an opening through the sea (the marshy Sea of Reeds) for the Israelites to pass through (Exod. 14:21-22). Deeper water on the sides of the passage form protecting walls against a flank attack (Exod. 14:22).

The Egyptian army follows the Israelites into the seabed. The soil that supports the people, though, is too soft for chariots. The wheels mire and clog, the troops try to flee, and the returning tides drown the army (Exod. 14:23-28). The Israelites are out of Egypt and into the wilderness of Shur (Exod. 15:22).

In the Egypt era of Hebrew history, there develops an awareness of the expansive sovereignty of God. During the patriarchal period, the sovereignty of God was believed to be primarily of a place and a people—Canaan and the "chosen" people of Abraham—whereas other places and other people were believed to be ruled by other gods. Their experience of living outside Canaan, in the lands of other gods, leads the Hebrews to believe that God watches over them there also. In the contest with the Pharaoh about leaving Egypt, the Israelites come to believe that their God is more powerful than the gods of Egypt. Belief in the larger realm of God's sovereignty leads eventually to belief in monotheism, or one universal infinite God.

The belief that a "line of promise" was divinely established to carry forward the clan headship and covenant relationship becomes a firm tenet of faith in the patriarchal period and continues—and even is enhanced—in the belief that God chooses the carrier of the line in each generation. This is revealed by Jacob's blessing of the sons of Joseph (Gen. 48:17-20), and in Jacob's blessing of his sons (Gen. 49:3-4, 8-10).

The Passover is established and declared to be a perpetual memorial to celebrate God's deliverance of Israel from Egypt (Exod. 13:3-10). As a result of the Passover event, there develops the faith and practice that God has declared ownership of all Israelite firstborn sons and male animals (Exod. 13:1, 12-15) and that they are to be sacrificed or redeemed by substitute sacrifice. Sons cannot be sacrificed—God had prevented the sacrifice of Isaac by Abraham—so a lamb is to be the substitute for a son. A more valuable animal could be redeemed by the sacrifice of a lesser valuable animal, a lamb instead of a donkey (Exod. 13:13). This belief in substitute sacrifice is a continuing tenet. In the New Testament, substitute sacrifice becomes the basis for believing that the crucifixion of Jesus is a substitute blood sacrifice to cleanse the guilt of Adam's original sin (Rom. 3:24-25, 5:9).

Revelation of the divine name, *YaHWeH*, becomes established and sacred, even too sacred for humans to speak. The Israelites use the address, *Adhonai* (Lord), to refer to God, and later combine the two into a hybrid word *Jehovah*, which appears often in the Hebrew scriptures/Old Testament.

The Journey to Sinai

After the exodus deliverance the Israelites do not head straight toward Canaan: "God did not lead them by way of the land of the Philistines" (Exod. 13:13). Although this is the short, direct way to the promised land, along by the southeast corner of "The Great Sea" (Mediterranean), the Philistines control the area and are a warring people. By taking an alternate route, the Israelites can avoid the danger that the people "would repent…and return to Egypt" (Exod. 13:17).

Instead, they head southeast toward Sinai, a way familiar to Moses. Not all is smoothness and ease, however. The area is arid, and water and food are very scarce. It is a harsh contrast to the well-watered, fertile Land of Goshen. The people complain (Exod. 15:24), and blame Moses and Aaron (Exod. 16:2), so the Lord provides manna and sends quail (Exod. 16:4, 13).

The journey takes the Israelites three months to travel from the exodus site to Sinai (a 200-mile trip). There they camp for almost a year (Exod. 19:1, Num. 10:11-12).

The Significance of Sinai

The Israelites believe their escape from slavery is a divine deliverance. At Sinai they experience life-changing and long-lasting events. The people arrive there as loosely related tribes of former slaves, needing everything from organizational structure, to guidance for how to survive in an arid wilderness, to a religious system and training. The leaders face the complex tasks of creating order within the tribes, establishing regulations for their civic activities and relationships, developing plans for their nomad life through a wilderness toward a promised land, and defining their obligations for religious practices to maintain obedience to their covenant God.

At the beginning, Moses attempts to carry the total responsibility by having every decision come to him (Exod.18:13). His father-in-law wisely warns him of the need to share the load, however (Exod. 18:14-23), so group leaders are assigned and delegated responsibilities.

Moses begins to spend periods of time on the mountain in communion with God (Exod. 19:3, 20; 24:1-2; 34:2-4). In fact, he stays on the mountain so much that the people despair (Exod. 24:12-14; 32:1). They insist that Aaron make a golden calf idol to go before them, which makes God angry. But Moses entreats God for the people, and God's anger is assuaged (Exod. 32:11-14). The Israelites will, nevertheless, suffer a plague (Exod. 32:35). God threatens to abandon them, and send them to Canaan on their own (Exod. 33:3), but Moses appeals to God's covenant promises (Exod. 33:12-16) and God relents (Exod. 33:17-20).

The Sinai story spans from arrival (Exod. 19:1) till departure (Num. 10:11). The intervening text, except for narrative passages, is written as though it is made up of instructions given to Moses on the mountain and then delivered by Moses to the people.

Convincing evidence exists that the Old Testament documents in their current form were compiled centuries later during and after the Babylonian Exile. The Levitical scribes who fulfilled that momentous task used the oral traditions that had developed from Abraham onward, and any written fragments available to them. I dare suggest, therefore, that what actually develops at Sinai is the necessary "order and instructions" for the tribes to survive and follow on the journey from Sinai forward.

The religious leaders—Moses, Aaron, the Aaronic priests, and the Levitical scribes—have to interpret the Sinai instructions, and make inferences for matters not covered, through eight centuries from Sinai to Babylon. Their interpretations and suppositions become the extensive Mosaic legislation contained in our Old Testament, including the laws of civic order, the rules of moral behavior, the dietary guidance for healthy survival, and the religious requirements and practices for faithful obedience to God. Significant changes develop through the ongoing centuries in all areas covered by the Mosaic legislation.

It should be noted that Deuteronomy 31:24-26, the sentence about Moses "writing down in a book the words of this law...," is a misleading translation. The Hebrew word for "book" translates to "a writing," which for Moses would have been on a stone, a clay tablet, or an animal skin. Making books of stacked leaves, as we mean by the word "book," was not invented until the Romans started the process in the first century of the Christian era. Nevertheless, I am convinced that we owe an enormous debt of gratitude to those unknown and unnamed Levites who responded to the inspiring guidance of God and preserved the records of God's people from ancient origins for our knowledge and guidance.

The Origins of Mosaic Religion

Without a basic understanding of Mosaic influence, it is not possible to understand the ongoing development of Jewish religion or its influence on the Christian religion. The major civic and social change in the Egypt era is the evolution from a single patriarchal family into a tribal nation, a massive group of twelve families. In addition to the organizational, relationship, and physical survival requirements of these families, religious observances need to be defined and practiced to establish their obedient faithfulness to the "God of their fathers" who has delivered them from bondage.

Moses and the Israelites have inherited the covenant religion of their patriarchal ancestors. Vestiges of that covenant religion have survived in the treasured promises and hope that have come down to the Israelites who left Egypt in the Exodus. A "new beginning" results from the experience of Moses in the revelation of the personal name for God (I AM, *YHWH*), and from the guidance by God to Moses during the year of encampment at Sinai.

Some indication of a belief about God develops: "… the whole earth is mine…" (Exod. 19:5). This is a broadening advance from the polytheism of previous centuries. The tribes' belief about "their" God becomes greater and more supreme than the idol gods of other tribes.

The most significant new feature of Mosaic religion is the development of Tabernacle-centered religious practice, with an Ark of the Covenant as an object of devotion. The Tabernacle is designed for set-up and take-down as the Israelites move in the wilderness (Exod. 36:8-38). It is their established center of worship. The furnishings for the Tabernacle include a "most holy place" for the Ark, which is for them the place of God's presence among them (Exod. 25:21-30).

The two most significant features of the Ark are the cover (lid) and the intended contents. The cover is also "the mercy seat." Inside the "holy of holies," the mercy seat of the Ark is the place to which God will come to meet Moses and give commands and guidance for the people (Exod. 25:22). Inside the Ark is to be placed the "testimony" (Tables of the Law, Ten Commandments) (Exod. 25:21). Tradition develops that an omer of manna and Aaron's "rod that budded" are to be placed before the Ark, or in the Ark, as perpetual memorials of God's provision and guidance (Heb. 9:4, see Exod. 16:31-33, and Num. 17:8-10).

The Mosaic Sacrificial System

The central features of Tabernacle-centered religious practice consist of a table and bread affirming the presence of God (Exod. 25:30); a bronze altar for ritual sacrifices, hollow and probably filled with earth (Exod. 27:2, 8; 20:24); and an olive oil lamp to burn continually in the sacred court surrounding the Tabernacle (Exod. 27:9, 20).

> The original Sinai ritual details cannot be distinguished with certainty within the complex array of ritual requirements that evolve by the time of the Temple destruction by the Babylonian sack of Jerusalem in 586 BCE. Nevertheless, it is clear that the Tabernacle, Ark, and some of the related ritual sacrifices are entirely new features of Israelite religion. They will develop with greater complexity through the centuries by priestly and scribal interpretation, amplification, and additions.

The Mosaic rituals call for offerings to be presented in two forms, animal and cereal/vineyard (Lev. 1:2, 2:1), and within these are various types:

- *Sacrificial*—well-being (peace, shalom) (Lev. 7:11) and guilt (Lev. 5:5, 7:1): Peace offerings begin at Sinai as private sacrifices, but later develop into communal offerings on behalf of the total Israelite people.

- *Peace*—thank (Lev. 7:12), votive, and free will (Lev. 7:16): Thank offerings are presented as expressions of gratitude to God for divine blessings received (Lev. 3:1-2, 7:11-13). Votive offerings are given when making a vow of some special kind to God (Lev. 7:16). Freewill offerings are tendered if a person simply wants to express general joy at being cared for and blessed by God (Lev. 7:16).

- *Guilt*—unintentional breach of faith (Lev. 5:15) and sin (Lev. 6:25–7:7): Sin offerings, made for individuals (Lev. 1:2) and for the entire congregation (Lev. 4:13), are sacrifices made to express guilt for unwitting errors and sinful acts, and to seek forgiveness from God.

> Not all sinfulness is believed to be in the same rank of evil. Psalm 51:1-2 has three words describing sinfulness: Sin (*HaTaTh*) is a simple misstep or mistake (Lev. 4:1, 13). Transgression (*PhaSha*) is deliberate, intentionally wrong action (Lev. 6:1-7). Iniquity (*AWaN*) is rooted in deeply corrupt character (Lev. 26:14-15, 40-43; Num. 15:30-31).
>
> The sin offering for atonement becomes the most central "sin offering for all the people" in the Day of Atonement once each year. Specific regulations of required ritual procedures are set forth for the high priest, the Tabernacle, the Ark, and the people (Leviticus 16).
>
> The central significance of "atonement" in Israelite (and Christian) religion calls for careful study. The practice of "sacrificing a substitute" developed through the Exodus experience in which a lamb is slain, its blood is placed on the doors of Hebrews, and the plague of death "passes over" the Hebrew houses and their "firstborn" are spared while all the firstborn of

the Egyptians die (Exod. 12:3-7, 12-13). The substitute sacrifice tenet of faith becomes established in Israel. All firstborns, human or beast, belong to God (Exod. 13:1). They must be redeemed or destroyed (Exod. 13:12-13). Belief is that God will accept a substitute lamb sacrifice instead of death of a son or a valued animal.

As the Mosaic system of ritual sacrifices develops, a substitute sacrifice for the penalty of sin becomes central in "the day of atonement." It involves both the sacrifice of a goat and a ram, and the sending of a scapegoat into the wilderness to perish (Lev. 16:5-6, 15-16, 20-22, 27-28). The Day of Atonement is decreed to be an annual observance (Lev. 16:29-31).

The meaning of substitutionary ritual sacrifice is central in Israelite religious history. The basic root word translated "to atone" is *KiPeR*, which means "to cover over." The use of "atone" to translate *KiPeR* is problematic. Atone was first used as an English word in 1513 CE, just in time to be used in the King James Bible where it is used to translate *KiPeR*. That is a misleading translation. The original meaning of atone came from Middle English "at+one," meaning "to be reconciled." The "reconciliation" meaning has become declared obsolete, and the preferred meaning has become specifically "to reconcile God to man through the sacrificial death of Jesus Christ."[1]

The dictionary describes an evolution of meaning to fit theological development, but that does not remove the problem. *KiPeR* is used widely in Mosaic teaching to describe the process of sprinkling the blood of a sacrificed animal before and on the Ark and Mercy Seat inside the Holy Place on the Day of Atonement, to cover over the sins and guilt of disobedience for the Israelites: sacrificed blood expiates their guilt (pays the penalty for and erases the guilt of those offenses), to gain forgiveness from God (Lev. 16:6, 11, 15-16, 30).

This expiation is considered by the people to be an act on their part, offering a substitute instead of themselves to suffer the penalty due for their sinfulness. They believe God will accept their covering over their sins with the sacrificial blood, and will approve the sending away of those sins on the scapegoat into the wilderness to perish (see Ps. 103:12).

Key questions are raised by this ritual practice as it relates to the human understanding of the meaning of religion:

- How is the sin problem of humanity resolved in the relationship between God and humanity?
- Does the resolving take place on God's side or on the human side?
- Does the resolving come about by satisfying the just demands of God that appropriate penalty be paid for guilt before forgiveness will be granted?
- Can an appropriate penalty be paid by substituting the sacrifice of another—an animal, for instance?

This tenet of faith in Israelite belief that substitute blood sacrifice expiates sinful guilt became the basis in Christian theology for a tenet of faith that

God paid the substitute penalty for human sin by the shed blood of Jesus in crucifixion.

Biblical records reflect clearly that development took place in human beliefs about atonement. *KiPeR* is used to describe paying a penalty to satisfy an offending action, as in Abimelech's gifts to Abraham to compensate him for having taken Sarah into Abimelech's harem (Gen. 20:16). When Jacob hopes to gain peace with Esau by sending gifts before their meeting, he thinks, "I may appease him (cover his face and assuage his anger) with the present ..." (Gen. 32:20-21).

As time passes and the regulations for sin offerings become more detailed and complex, the meaning of the atonement rituals tend to become more symbolic and spiritualized. The moral responsibility of the people becomes more a required part of the process of becoming right with God. By the time of the 8th-century BCE prophets, the moral requirements for acceptance with God become equal to, or more important than, the ritual sacrifices (See Isa. 1:11-17, Amos 5:21-24, Mic. 6:6-8).

The Mosaic rituals are central to Israelite religion for about six centuries. They are practiced at the Tabernacle, and at consecrated high places (see Num. 23:1-4, 1 Sam. 9:12, 1 Kgs. 3:2-4) until Solomon builds the Temple in Jerusalem. The Mosaic ritual practice is then centered in the Jerusalem Temple until the city and Temple are destroyed by the Babylonians in 586 BCE.

A Mosaic Summary

The Hebrew/Israelite religion evolved through the patriarchal and tribal periods. With Abraham's "new beginning," the Hebrew people believe that the generic deity (*El*, The Supreme Being) who has called him is one of numerous tribal deities who compete for control over local areas and groups of people. They early come to believe that their God has sovereignty over Canaan and has chosen them to be his people, living there, worshipping him exclusively, and obeying his commands. As nomads, they practice building altars wherever they reside and offer sacrifices to their God.

The Hebrews who migrate to Egypt understand religion to mean that God has made a covenant with Abraham and his family and descendants. Their responsibility in the covenant is to worship God only and to obey his commands. God's part is his promise that if they will be faithfully obedient as his exclusive people, he will bless them and make them prosper.

The era of Egyptian residence and enslavement ends when God acts to deliver his people by calling Moses to lead them out of Egypt. This historic event involves God sending overwhelming plagues on Egypt until they are willing for the Israelites to "plunder the Egyptians" and make a start toward freedom (Exod. 12:30-36). The plagues, the Passover, and the passage through the sea are lasting evidences that the Israelites' God is superior to the gods of Egypt, and that they are the people chosen by God to be the recipients of his favor and blessing.

Belief about the presence of God becomes more specifically detailed after the Exodus. Under the leadership of Moses, the Israelites believe that God establishes a definite way by which he will make his presence known and how he will communicate with them.

After they leave Egypt and before they reach Sinai, while in the arid semi-desert, complaining about scarcity of food and water, they sense God appearing to them in a cloud (Exod. 16:10). When they arrive at Sinai, the crest of the mountain becomes the place of presence to which Moses goes to meet God and receive commands for the people (Exod. 19:3, 9, 16-20).

While the Israelites camp at Sinai, while waiting for the Tabernacle to be built, the peak of Sinai with its cloud and fire or the tent of meeting are the places of God's contact with them. The people continue to believe that God dwells in the heavens, but comes to the mountain or the tent to give his guiding commands to Moses for them. As with Abraham, most of the records simply read "God said," but the assumption is clear, even when it is not stated, that Moses is with God on the mountain or in the tent when the message is received (Exod. 24:15-17, 34:2-8).

Under the impetus of what they believe are God's specific commands, Moses sets forth the beginning of an organized system of ritual sacrifices and offerings as the basis of their religious practices to faithfully obey the Lord. He tells them that sacrifices can be offered only at the Tabernacle ("Temple") with its Ark, for that is where God has chosen as the place of his presence among them (Exod. 26:33-34, 40:34-35; Lev. 17:2-9; Deut. 12:13).

When the Tabernacle is finished and set up (Exod. 40:1-33), the cloud which has come to the crest of the mountain covers the tent and the glory of the Lord fills the Tabernacle (Exod. 40:34.) The presence of the Lord becomes for the Israelites "in the Tabernacle." God still "fills the heavens," but he comes among them to the Most Holy Place and there manifests his presence by the cloud to guide them (Exod. 40:36-38; Lev. 16:2; Num. 9:15-23, 10:11-13; Deut.1:31-33).

The limitation of sacrifices to one central location proves to be a problem after they are settled in the eleven regions of Canaan and east of the Jordan. Exceptions have to be made. Those who are distant from the location of the Tabernacle are permitted to eat the meat of sacrificed animals in their home places, but burnt offerings and offerings of blood are to be taken and offered at the Tabernacle (Deut. 12:20-28).

The most significant tenet of faith that develops within the Tabernacle and ritual sacrifice system of Mosaic religion is the doctrine of atonement, based on the belief that God requires justification before forgiveness. Justice as a feature of God's character becomes a tenet of Israelite faith going forward. (It becomes problematic for Jews when the Temple with its altar for expiating blood sacrifice is destroyed and the sacrifices cannot be offered.

The tenet of faith about God's character requiring justification will need to be considered later in Christian faith.)

The development of Mosaic faith and practice is the most significant and long-lasting feature of Jewish religion, after the call and covenant with Abraham, and until the transforming changes that occur during and after the Babylonian Exile.

Note

[1] Merriam-Webster, *Collegiate Dictionary*, 10th ed. (Springfield, MA: Merriam-Webster, Inc., 1999), 73b.

Chapter 3
Religion in the Kingdom Period

The tribal period of life in Canaan (1400/1250–1050 BCE) was not a settled or peaceful time due to the constant competition and periodic conflict between tribes. In addition, an aggressive and warring people, the Philistines, had established themselves in the southwest area along the Mediterranean coast (Exod. 13:17). A seafaring and trading people, the Phoenicians had also settled in the northwest along the coast. The competition and conflict never allowed the Israelites to live unchallenged in what they believed to be their divinely gifted homeland.

Public sentiment developed for the formation of a kingdom that could unite their resources against the non-Israelite inhabitants (1 Sam. 8:5–12:25). The kingdom period then spans from the anointing of Saul as king (1050 BCE) until the destruction of Jerusalem and Judah by the Babylonians just after the beginning of the 6th century BCE. During this period significant changes occur in the national, social, and religious life of the Israelite people

The Reigns of Saul, David, and Solomon

The judge/prophet Samuel opposes anointing a king, but the people insist. Samuel relents, but with a stark warning, and then anoints Saul (1 Sam. 10:1). Saul is placed in authority (1 Sam. 12:13, 13:1), and reigns until he is killed by Philistines in battle (1 Sam. 31:1-6).

Saul's reign is troubled but effective. Before the establishment of the kingdom, the tribes were loosely related but largely lived as separate tribes in the areas assigned by Moses and Joshua when they arrived in Canaan. They are never able to "possess all the land," as they believe God has promised it to them (Deut. 7:2, 9:3, 20:17). They live intermingled with Canaanite tribes, sometimes in peace and sometimes at war—the stories of which are recorded in the book of Judges. They ask for a king to combine their strength so they can be more effective against those adversary peoples (1 Sam. 8:19-20).

Establishing a kingdom begins the process of uniting the twelve tribes into a nation. Saul does not rule as Samuel believes he should (1 Sam. 13:13-14), so under what he believes are God's instructions, Samuel anoints David to become king (1 Sam. 16:1-13). Saul's jealousy and conflict with David continue from that time until Saul is killed in battle (1 Sam. 31:1-6).

After the death of Saul there begins a struggle between the supporters of Saul and the forces of David (2 Sam. 3:1), until David prevails at Hebron and becomes king over Judah (2 Sam. 2:3-4). First, David reigns over the southern tribes at Hebron for seven years, after which the other tribes yield and accept David as king over all Israel (2 Sam. 5:1-5). The golden age of Israelite history begins.

David's victories in battle enable him to gain control of the Jebusite stronghold of Zion and establish it as his city (2 Sam. 5:6-10). Jerusalem becomes the religious center for Israelite/Jewish life. David brings the Ark to Jerusalem and establishes it there as the Jewish center of religious devotion (2 Sam. 6:1-17). He wants to build a Temple for the Ark to replace "the tent" in which it is located, but his years of conflict and battle to secure the kingdom against all its adversary opponents make this move impossible. He is assured by God that his kingdom will be secure and his son will build the Temple (2 Sam. 7:9-13). Solomon does build the Temple with all its magnificence, and places the Ark and Tabernacle securely there with all the sacred furnishings. The glory of God is manifest there as "the cloud" fills the Temple (1 Kgs. 8:1-11).

The reigns of David and Solomon, along with the construction of the Temple, bring new features to Israelite religion. The changes are not so much in tenets of their faith as they are in concepts of grandeur. Whereas Abraham believed God is a God of wandering nomads, and Moses believed God is a God of wilderness journeys and tribal struggles, Israelites during the kingdom era believe that God is a God of national prominence and majesty.

David begins the process of making Jerusalem a "royal" city (2 Sam. 5:9-13), and then Solomon expands the grandeur of the royal city (1 Kgs. 3:1, 4:22-24, 9:1, 10:4-8) and his own prominence (1 Kgs. 7:1-12). The national stature of Israel, the grandeur of Jerusalem, the magnificence of the Temple, and the royal court of their king lead the Israelites to think differently about "their" God. As the Israelites become familiar with earthly kings living in palatial splendor within courts of grandeur, they begin to attribute the same features of royal magnificence to God.

The Psalms, which come largely from the kingdom era, reflect images of God "enthroned in the heavens" with a host of angels surrounding, praising, and serving him (Ps. 11:4; 103:19-20; 123:1; 148:2, 13). With the presence of the Temple, the celebration of feasts and festival seasons becomes much more prominent as features of Jewish worship, whereas worship during the tribal era focused on the Tabernacle and ritual sacrifices and offerings and the way they affect relationships with God.

It is also during the kingdom era that morality is raised to new importance by the development of the prophetic movement. Upright living, in addition to faithful ritual performance, is a major theme of prophets such as Nathan who confronts David personally (2 Sam. 12:1-15). The great 8th-century prophets call for godly living in their preaching to the nation (Isa. 1:4-20, Hos. 4:1-3, Amos 1:2–5:24, Mic. 6:6-8). Mosaic legislation is centered on justice and kindness between people and ritual faithfulness in obedience to God. In the prophetic movement, religious faithfulness becomes more personalized with emphasis on individual conduct in addition to national values.

The Divided Kingdom

The fortunes of national Israel decline during four centuries following the reign of Solomon. First, the kingdom divides as a result of Solomon's excesses and the arrogance of his son Rehoboam (1 Kgs. 12:1-17, 25-33). A southern kingdom, Judah, stays with the royal line of David/Solomon. A northern kingdom, Israel, separates to follow Jeroboam. The national fortunes of the two kingdoms vary thereafter.

Neither of the smaller kingdoms can stand against the empires that rise, compete, and successively decline. Alliances abound. Imperial armies from Egypt, Assyria, Babylon, and Persia rise and fall in the area during the next six centuries. Periods of conflict move back and forth across the "land bridge" of the two Israelite kingdoms.

In the late 8th century (722 BCE) the Assyrian Empire destroys the Northern Kingdom, and its ten tribes become the "lost tribes." That fate results from intermarriage with Assyrians by Israelites taken to Assyria, where they are lost by assimilation. Intermarriage with occupying Assyrians and Canaanites by Israelites not taken to Assyria results in a mixed-race called Samaritans in the Northern Kingdom area. The Northern Kingdom ceases to exist, and that area continues under Assyrian control until the Babylonian empire arises to replace Assyria.

The Southern Kingdom continues until the 6th century (586 BCE) when the Babylonians conquer it, sack Jerusalem, destroy the Temple, and take the elite of the nation into Babylonian captivity. That becomes a continuing story.

Religion in a Time of Imperial Change

The division of the Israelite nation into two nations brings about a realignment of the religious institutions. Jerusalem, located in the Southern Kingdom, continues to be the religious center of Judah. The religious situation in the Northern Kingdom is very different.

After the revolt led by Jeroboam, he is crowned king (1 Kgs. 12:20). To keep his subjects from having ties to the Temple in Jerusalem, Jeroboam sets up golden calves at Bethel in the south of Israel and at Dan in the north of the nation (1 Kgs. 12:26-29) and worship sites on "high places" (1 Kgs. 12:31). Religion in Israel becomes corrupted from its Israelite heritage. Jeroboam only appoints priests who are not Levites and establishes new festivals (1 Kgs. 12:31-33).

Israel is ruled by a series of kings. The capital is moved about by the kings until it is finally settled at Samaria. Culture and religion are corrupted, with the worst religious corruption represented by Ahab and his wife Jezebel who establish temples and altars to Baal and Asherah in Samaria (1 Kgs. 16:30-34, 18:19).

In tracing the meaning of religion through the ages of human social and national development, it is clearly illustrated in historical events that people will use religion to gain power, and once in power, use religion to sustain and enhance themselves in their positions of power. Consider these examples from the kingdom period of Jewish history:

- David moves the capital from Hebron in the south to Jerusalem, nearer the border between the southern and northern tribes, as he struggles with internal divisions to become king over all Israel (2 Sam. 2:10-11, 5:1-5).

- Jeroboam and his successors, as kings of the Northern Kingdom, use religious concerns of the people and even corrupt their religious heritage to influence the political struggle between the divided kingdoms.

- Solomon uses alliances made by marrying "foreign women" as he expands Israel's imperial influence (1 Kgs. 3:1-2). He honors their wishes (1 Kgs. 9:24), builds temples to their pagan gods, and shares with them in the worship of those gods (1 Kgs. 11:1-8).

- During the wars of the divided kingdom period, the Israelites choose to use the Ark as a fetish to seek the help of God in their battles (1 Sam. 4:3-4). On the other hand, they often choose political alliances instead of trust in God as they plan their military strategies.

A religious question is raised by the national struggles and imperial wars during the divided kingdom period: Does God personally and actively "manage" all the events that have to do with the rise and fall of nations and with the lives of individual persons (see Jer. 18:1-11, Acts 17:24-26, Rom. 9:20-24)? Biblical records show that people readily declare trust in God for the benefits of his "care and blessing." When crisis times arise, however, many are willing to trust "their own smarts" and act on their own. Throughout human history, that seems to be a widespread human trait.

In the early centuries of their history, the Hebrews'/Israelites' religious beliefs include features in their understanding of the character of God that are problematic. The Hebrews believe their God is sovereign over Canaan and, therefore, can take it from the native inhabitants and give it to them as a homeland (Gen. 12:7, 24:7, 48:3-4; Exod. 32:13). They believe that Canaan is God's land, but Canaanites are not God's people and thus have no right to be living on God's land. When the Israelites come out of Egypt, they believe they have a commandment from God to "drive out" all other tribes from Canaan and adjacent lands (Exod. 23:30-31, 34:11-12; Deut. 7:2, 9:3, 20:17). Their religious faith includes a mission to do total "ethnic cleansing" of the land to avoid any corrupting influence from those previous inhabitants (Deut. 7:2-5, 20:18).

This tenet of their faith has the Israelites believing that God approves of group annihilation. It seems reasonable to them because of the tribal culture of their era. They believe that deities have only local sovereignty over different people groups. (That belief, however, is certainly contrary to what later prophets will proclaim [Amos 1:3, 9, 11] and Jesus will teach [Matt. 5:38-45].)

The Emergence of Monotheism

The most significant religious change that develops before the Babylon/Persia era is the emergence of monotheism. During the patriarchal era when tribes believed in many local deities competing for sovereignty over land and people, the Hebrews only believed in one special God. With the passing of time, their belief in their God continued to expand.

They come to believe that his sovereignty is greater; that "all the earth" is his (Exod. 19:5). When they become a powerful nation with a great royal city, a Temple, and a king reigning in a court of splendid majesty, they attribute that same kind of majestic grandeur to God, raised to heavenly heights. Psalmists sing of God enthroned in the heavens with a court of angels surrounding and praising him (Ps. 11, 103, 123, 148). But in their belief, pagan people still have their pagan gods.

By the mid-8th century, marked changes are beginning: Polytheism is progressively giving way to monotheism. Tribalism is being replaced by nationalism. Knowledge about the natural world is developing. Among the Israelites, belief about their God is becoming more expansive, with his sovereignty covering both the earth and the heavens. Their beliefs about "competing deities" (pagan gods) are becoming more localized and diminished. They believe that any influence those gods have is beneath and subservient to the greater sovereignty of their God.

There is a hint of incipient monotheism in Deuteronomy 4:35, "…the Lord is God, there is no other besides him," and in verse 39 following. When Solomon dedicates the Temple, he prays, "…there is no God like you in heaven above or on earth beneath" (1 Kgs. 8:23). While he affirms the supreme sovereignty of God, he does not deny the existence of other deities. Psalm 82 describes God as sovereign above other gods in a heavenly council.

Forthright monotheism is expressed in Isaiah 44:6, "I am the first and I am the last, besides me there is no god." In the following paragraph (Isa. 44:9-17), the writer scornfully denies that any other deities exist. He declares that they are the products of human imagination, and that the graven images of those gods are simply the work of human hands. To put this development into historical context, it must be noted that this passage is in the Second Isaiah portion (chapters 40–55) of this document, which places this proclamation in the 6th century BCE when the Jewish kingdom era is ending under the assault of the Babylonian empire.

Jeremiah 10:1-16 expresses the same denial of any reality of deity except the universal sovereignty of God. The prophet affirms with praise the awesome greatness of Israel's God as the creator and sovereign of all the earth and the heavens. This prophet is also from the 6th century BCE.

The biblical records reveal clearly that, among the Hebrews/Israelites/Jews, from the 20th–6th centuries BCE, their belief about the existence and nature of deity develops from tribal polytheism to universal monotheism. The references cited, however, reflect the belief of prophetic voices only. It may surely be assumed that many, if not most, of the Jews would have still believed in pagan gods, and the temptation to idolatry would have only slowly faded away.

The national disaster of Babylonian destruction of Jerusalem with its Temple brings an end to the kingdom era. The elite of Judah are taken to exile in Babylon (2 Kgs. 24:10-16). The *am haaretz* (people of the land) of the nation are left to "make it on their own" under Babylonian dominance (2 Kgs. 25:12, 22-24). Some rebel and flee to Egypt to escape (2 Kgs. 25:25-26). The era of exile, followed by the Persian release from captivity and the remnant return to Judah, brings major changes to Jewish culture and religion.

Chapter 4
Religion in the Exile Period

The kingdom period of Israelite history, which began in 1040 BCE, ended with the Babylonian conquest of Judah in 587 BCE. Previously, in 722 BCE, Assyria had conquered Israel.

For those taken captive to Babylon, exile means separation from so much of what life has involved. They are 600 miles from their cherished home. Their beloved city Jerusalem with its magnificent Temple is in ruins. The ritual sacrifices that are so central to the Israelites' religion cannot be offered apart from the Temple in a foreign land. The exiles in Babylon are bereft. Psalm 137 voices for them their depth of desolation: "How could we sing the Lord's song in a foreign land?" (v. 4).

Although the exiles have lost much, they are permitted to maintain their Jewish culture and practice their religion. The governor in Judah counsels the remainder left behind to cooperate with the Chaldean officials (2 Kgs. 25:24, Jer. 40:7-12). Jeremiah sends a letter to the exiles in Babylon and urges them to live as normally as possible, to cooperate with the Babylonians, and to look forward to "going home" (Jer. 29:1-10).

The Babylonian story is only the beginning of the Exile narrative. In 539 BCE the Persian army conquers Babylon. The Persian king, Cyrus, issues an edict a year later that releases the Jews from exile and permits them to return to Judah (2 Chron. 36:22-23, Ezra 1:1-4). The story of "remnant return(s)" is a mixed story.

A zealous group goes very soon and begins to rebuild (Ezra 1:5-8, 3:10-13), but adversaries arise to oppose them and force a halt to work on the city and the Temple (Ezra 4:1-4, 23-24). Haggai and Zechariah appeal to Darius, the new Persian king, who recovers Cyrus' edict and orders the work to resume (Ezra 5:1-2; 6:8-9, 12). The small replacement Temple is completed some five years later (Ezra 6:14-15). Groups of exiles and their descendants continue to return to Palestine for another century to live there under Persian control.

Religious Development

The central belief that has characterized the Israelites' religion since the call of Abraham, that they are the covenant people of the God who has chosen them, continues to be fundamental. The developed system of rituals and sacrifices established by Moses and expanded through the centuries is set forth in their treasured Torah traditions. Their faith in their exclusive relationship with God has become centered in the Temple, with the Ark as the physical representation of God's presence among them. The destruction of the Temple and the exile from Jerusalem creates an immediate crisis for them in Babylon. How can the exiles continue to practice their religion and pay homage to God? How can they preserve their Torah traditions scattered throughout the land in small subject groups?

One prominent distinctly Jewish religious development, following the destruction of the nation of Judah, is the emerging feature of messianic hope. Hebrew/Israelite life and religion have always been theocratic-centered. The Jewish people believe God has called, led, cared for, and established leaders, and that God has reigned in sovereignty over them.

Anointing with oil is practiced as a ritual of consecration, setting apart an individual for the service of God as a priest or king. Anointing is believed to make a person or thing (Ark, altar, dish, building) clean, pure, and devoted, and thus fit for the service of God. Israelite kings are referred to as "the Lord's anointed" (*messiah*) (1 Sam. 24:10, 2 Sam. 19:21, Ps. 2:2).

The identification of "anointed king" with "messiah" ("an anointed one") has been part of Israel's history/religion since before the end of the kingdom era with the destruction of Jerusalem/Judah in 586 BCE. This king/messiah identification begins with the dream for a new king (David?) and a new era (David's reign?), and the dream becomes a "messianic hope" during the Exile and afterward.

Two streams of messianic hope develop, both centered in the restoration of an earthly kingdom, ruled over from Jerusalem by a new son of David. One stream believes and hopes for an "anointed" king who will be a mighty warrior. With God's blessing, this king will vanquish all adversaries, regather scattered Jews, and establish a mighty kingdom of Jewish prosperity (Isa. 9:4-5; Psalm 110; Hag. 2:6-9, 20-23; Zech. 9:1-8).

The other stream of belief and hope is for an "anointed" king who will establish a Jewish kingdom that will, with God's blessing, become the center of a new world of universal peace (Isa. 2:1-4, 42:1-9; Jer. 23:5-6, 33:15-22; Ezek. 17:22-24, 37:21-28).

References to messianic hope in the Old Testament texts are primarily about hope for the divine restoration of an Israelite kingdom, a re-gathering of scattered Israelites, the defeat of adversary nations, and national prosperity. Restoration of the Davidic dynasty is a central feature for hope of a recovery of the "golden age" of David's reign.

During the postexilic period and into the Christian era, messianic belief and hope focus primarily on end-time tenets of faith (see the apocalyptic vision in Dan. 7:9-14). A Jewish source says that "Messiah as a designation of the eschatological personality does not exist in the Old Testament."[1] Commenting on the royal marriage in Psalm 45, E. McNeil Poteat writes "... the ideal picture of the messiah-conqueror and ruler who, as the political fortunes of the Jews declined, more and more possessed their imaginations."[2] More about messianic faith will be appropriate in consideration of New Testament passages.

Religion in the Exile Period

Three other features of postexilic Judaism describe changes that develop during and after the Exile: the synagogue, religious leadership, and the influence of Persian religion.

The Synagogue

The Tabernacle/Temple with its altars has been a religious center where sacrifices and offerings are made to express their worship and to fulfill their obligations of gratitude and commitment, and for atonement. Sacrifices cannot be offered in Babylon. The specific historical origin of the synagogue cannot be established, but after the Exile it becomes a primary religious institution for Jews.

The synagogue is an institution for teaching, training, prayer, and worship, but not a place for offering sacrifices. Its leader is a rabbi (a teacher), not a priest (a performer of sacrifices). It seems certain that the synagogue is established by exiles to preserve Mosaic teachings and to provide a place of worship in Babylon. (In modern Judaism, temple and synagogue are used as practical synonyms, but animal sacrifice has not been a part of Jewish practice since the destruction of the Jerusalem Temple in 70 CE.)

Religious Leadership

Judah's religious leaders are among the groups taken to Babylon for control and to avoid uprisings (2 Kgs. 24:10-16, 25:18). A large number of them are recorded among those who return (Neh. 7:6, 39-45), including Ezra who is committed to study and teach the law (Ezra 7:1, 6, 10).

The Exile brings a crisis for the religious faith and practice of the Jews. Their faith in Canaan as a homeland gift from God is in jeopardy. The practice of the ritual sacrifices they trust for their "rightness with God" is denied them by destruction of the Temple and exile from Jerusalem. The priests and Levites in Babylon find themselves at the center of that religious crisis. They respond with a central commitment to find ways to preserve their Mosaic heritage.

Two developments reflect this commitment: the synagogue as a major Jewish religious institution and the production of Jewish historic oral traditions into written documents.

Some written documents existed in preexilic Israel. Moses is recorded to have written the beginnings of the law in a book (a writing) (Deut. 31:24). A "book of the law" becomes the basis for a revival under Josiah in Judah during the last years of the 7th century BCE (2 Kgs. 22:3-13). When the priest Ezra returns to Jerusalem from Babylon, he brings with him the "law of God" (writing, book, scroll) (Ezra 7:12-14, Neh. 8:8). Additionally, major editorial work on the entire Old Testament canonical documents is done during the exilic and postexilic periods. Textual studies and the language used support this conclusion.

The Hebrew language develops among the Semitic languages from Akkadian in the 12th-10th centuries BCE. As a spoken language, which would have been used in oral tradition, it is largely replaced by Aramaic by the end of the Exile. The dialect of Hebrew that has come down to us in the Old Testament is a literary language (rabbinic Hebrew, classical Hebrew) used primarily in written documents. It is prominent from the late 8th century through the postexilic period.[3] This supports the belief that centuries of oral tradition are edited into written form to ensure preservation by the work of scribes during and after the Exile. I believe this is a product of divine inspiration to those priests and scribes, and is an enormous gift to us.

There is a feature of this major editorial work that is a subject unto itself. It has to do with Genesis 1–11. The stories recorded are about pre-Hebrew history. However, they give no hint about their source and are not referred to in the documents of the Old Testament after Genesis 11, and not at all by Jesus. They give every evidence of having been composed from legend, folklore, reasoning, and inspiration as an introduction to the beginning of their accumulated oral traditions. As such, they become a part of postexilic Judaism.

The stories are vitally important because they become the basis for the tenets of original sin and universal human destiny to perdition. Those tenets of faith are central to the theology of Paul in the New Testament book of Romans

The Influence of Persian Religion

The Exile ends with the edict of release by Cyrus of Persia, but the influence of the Exile does not end with that political and civic release. The remnant returns are partial and extend over numerous decades. Significant Persian influence develops among the Jews who spend years among them. The most important religious influence is the Jewish exposure to the Persian religion Zoroastrianism. New and different tenets of faith develop in postexilic Judaism.

The dates of Zarathustra/Zoroaster's life, and the development of the Zoroastrian religion, are uncertain (1000–500 BCE). Two features of that religion are very important for our understanding of postexilic Judaism. One is the belief in monotheism.

Faith in forthright monotheism is developing among Jewish prophets. Isaiah 44:9-17 is widely believed to be exilic, and Jeremiah 10:3-10 surely comes from the Exile era. Monotheism is also becoming established in Persia in the form of Zoroastrianism.

Zoroastrianism includes belief in a single deity. The Persians name their supreme god *Ahura Mazda* ("The Wise Lord"). Zoroaster denies the existence of other gods, but as in Israelite Canaan other polytheistic religions are practiced in Persia. The developing belief in monotheism is common to both

Judaism and Zoroastrianism. This is not an entirely new tenet of faith for the Jews.

The Persian belief about the source of evil is quite different, however. Zoroaster introduces the idea of a demonic demigod, less than fully divine, but an evil force behind the problem of evil in the world. The Persians name this evil force *Angra Mainyu* ("The Evil Spirit"). Later, The Evil Spirit comes to be known also by the name *Shaitin* ("The Adversary") to describe his nature and activity in opposition to "The Wise Lord."[4]

This Zoroastrian tenet of faith represents a major change from preexilic Jewish religion. From its origin with Abraham, a great tradition of the Jewish religion is that both good and bad come from their God—favorable blessing if they are obedient and faithful, punitive and corrective chastisement if they are disobedient and unfaithful. I describe this tenet as moral monism, or good and bad originating from a single source. Zoroastrianism is, by contrast, dualistic: The Wise Lord and The Evil Spirit are responsible for good or bad in the world and in people's lives. I describe this tenet of faith as moral dualism. At least some of the exiles embrace moral dualism.

In addition to the belief in monotheism, in postexilic Judaism a doctrine of evil develops that identifies a "fallen angel" named *Satan* (Hebrew, "The Adversary"), whose nature and activity are in opposition to God.[5] Four Old Testament passages use the Satan reference:

- Psalm 109:6 refers to a human, and the Hebrew word is correctly translated "Accuser."
- 1 Chronicles 21:1 has Satan inciting David to "number Israel." (Also see 2 Samuel 24:1, which records that it was the Lord who "incited" David to do the numbering).
- Job 1:6-2:7 describes Satan in an adversary role as he challenges God about Job's faithfulness.
- Zechariah 3:1-2 is part of a prophetic vision about the building of a new Temple by the returning exiles. (Satan serves in an "adversary role," accusing the high priest who is a part of that restoration, but Satan is rebuked by God.)

This brief textual evidence by no means indicates that the moral dualism of Zoroastrianism is fully embraced by the returning exiles. It does, however, by time period and language similarity suggest a certain likelihood of kinship. By the beginning of the New Testament era, the dual morality tenet and the role of Satan are carried over into the developing Christian faith.By the beginning of the New Testament era, the dual morality tenet and the role of Satan are carried over into the developing Christian faith.

The returning Jews focus on rebuilding Jerusalem and the Temple, and reestablishing the Temple-centered sacrificial system of their Mosaic religious heritage. Cyrus authorizes the restoration of the Temple, and a remnant of released exiles set out to complete the lengthy and involved process (Ezra 1:2-11, Neh. 2:1-8).

The book of Ezra records that Zerubbabel is among the first group that, between 538–516 BCE, returns and builds a Temple (Ezra 1:1, 2:2, 6:15). Records of another returning group are found in the book of Nehemiah.

Nehemiah is concerned that the walls of Jerusalem have not been rebuilt. It takes twelve years to obtain permission and overcome opposition (Neh. 5:14), but the work of building is reported to take fifty-two days (Neh. 6:15). A dedication of the rebuilt walls (Neh. 12:27-47) is followed by a time of reform under Nehemiah's leadership (Neh. 13:6-31). Temple-centered Mosaic religion is reestablished in Jerusalem. The Ark is not recovered, however.

Notes

[1] "Messiah, Second Temple Period," https://www.jewishvirtuallibrary.org/messiah (accessed June 28, 2021).

[2] E. McNeil Poteat, "Psalms, Exposition," *The Interpreter's Bible*, vol. 4 (New York: Abingdon Press, 1955), 236-237.

[3] "Hebrew Language, Biblical Hebrew," https://en.wikipedia.org/wiki/Hebrew_language#Classical_Hebrew (accessed June 28, 2021).

[4] Lewis M. Hopfe and Mark R. Woodward, *Religions of the World* (Upper Saddle River, NJ: Pearson/Prentice Hall, 2005), 224-230.

[5] The identification of Satan as a "fallen angel" is based on Isaiah 14:12 (Lucifer, Day Star) and the noncanonical book 2 Enoch 29:3, and is cited in 2 Peter 2:4. This identification is not widely believed to be well-founded. See also Morgan P. Noyes, "The Snare of the Devil," *The Interpreter's Bible*, vol. 11 (New York: Abingdon Press, 1955), 414b.

Chapter 5
Learning from the Life and Teachings of Jesus

Persian dominance controlled the near-eastern region from its ascendancy in 539 BCE until it was displaced by the rising Greek empire. Alexander the Great defeated Darius III and finally ended the era of Persian empire dominance. Alexander died in 323 BCE, and the empire fell apart as his generals fought over control.

Beginning in the late 2nd century BCE, Judea becomes independent of foreign control until the Romans come in to subjugate them again in 63 BCE. These two and a half centuries are marked by struggle against foreign forces and influence, by cultural change and civil unrest, and by religious conflict and challenge. The synagogue movement continues to develop, but the Temple with its priestly hierarchy and its animal sacrifices is the central focus of Jerusalem religion. There are struggles between urban upper-class Jews who want to embrace Hellenist culture and dispense with Jewish rituals on one hand, and traditional Jews devoted to Mosaic religion on the other.

Roman control after 63 BCE establishes order again, but it is "occupied" order and "submission" is required. This politico-religious situation has been defined as a "domination system," characterized by political oppression, economic exploitation, and religious legitimation.[1] Rome is master, Judea is vassal, and the Jews live under the domination of both.

After the ritualizing of their religion by Moses, the priestly hierarchy of Aaron's descendants and the tribe of Levi dominate the interpretation, developmental expansion, and practice of Israelite/Jewish religion. With the defeat of Persia and the rise of Greece, the religious environment of Judea changes. The mystery and cult religions of Greece and Rome come onto the scene in Judea with their pantheons of gods. The most troubling "foreign" religion for the Jews is "emperor worship," which directly affects them by imperial decrees.

Jewish Temple worship flourishes. Festivals and accompanying pilgrimages are a prominent feature. The synagogue with its prayer and teaching services, led by rabbis, has developed widely across Judea. Synagogue worship thrives alongside, but apparently not in extensive competition, with the Temple and its ritual sacrifices presided over by priests. The dual morality adopted from Zoroastrianism, with Satan fostering evil in adversarial competition against God, has become an established tenet of faith in Judaism by the time Jesus is born.

The world into which Jesus is born is far different from the world in which Abraham and Moses, or David and Isaiah lived. Religion is different also. Culture and nations have developed through the centuries, and so has religion. Judaism of the 1st century CE is monotheistic, but challenged by Greek and Roman cultic religions, and especially by emperor worship. The people are less nomadic, more settled, and less rural, coming mainly from small towns and villages. Most of the people are peasants, but that does not mean destitute. Many, if not most, are small landowners or craftsmen. Those who own a plot of land cherish their heritage of a place they believe has come to them through the promise, gift, and leadership of God.

Jesus, too, grows up in a small town and works as a craftsman until he is thirty. He becomes an itinerant preacher/teacher for three years, and gains a following who believe him to be a wonder-worker and challenger of traditional Jewish religion. Influential people in both religion and politics oppose his teachings and his popularity with the peasant populace. They eventually scheme against him and secure his execution. The stories that fill out this picture are familiar to all who have been nurtured in Christian churches.

It is not the purpose of this writing to review those stories or to resolve the textual contradictions in them. Nor is it the purpose to join the conversation of textual scholars who search for the earliest and most accurate records of the life of Jesus and the origins of the Christian movement. I will begin at the baptism of Jesus, for that is where the teaching by Jesus begins. All of the records before his baptism come from other sources.

For context, let me affirm that I believe the Gospels are products of at least a long generation of developing faith and evolving traditions. For this writing, traditional texts of the Gospels will be used for the benefit of anyone who chooses to use this volume in personal Bible study. The remainder of this manuscript will focus on what I believe to be the most vital religious venture a person can undertake.

Nothing is more important than to have informed faith about the nature and character of the God one trusts and seeks to follow. It is equally important for every person to understand as best possible the meaning of being created in the image of God. Christian faith involves what it means to live in harmony with God or in alienation from God, what are the consequences of each quality of relationship, and how one's relationship with God can be made right and enhanced. The remainder of this chapter will seek to demonstrate what Jesus taught and practiced.

Learning from Jesus about God

The Gospels include four categories of teaching from Jesus about God: what Jesus says about the Father; what Jesus, as Eternal Son, reveals about God; what Jesus teaches in parables that reveal something about God; and what Jesus teaches about life that reveals approval or disapproval by God.

Learning from the Life and Teachings of Jesus

> The developed faith described in the Bible is the belief that God (the Supreme Being) is the Creator who conceives, designs, and brings into being physical matter, the universe, and all it contains (Ps. 24:1). God raises up a species called human persons. Each person has a physical body that has the nature of a mammalian animal, but also has a personal spirit/soul that is created in the image of God (Gen. 1:27).
>
> In the design of the physical universe, God established natural laws that determine the order and function of all material things, for example, the structure and energy of atoms and the laws of gravity, heat and cold, and movement. In the realm of spirit, God also established qualities of character and moral laws that determine human likeness to or variance from the character of God. A person's character either enhances or degrades human life and relationships.

Speaking about God, Jesus says that God is spirit (John 4:24). Describing what God as spirit is like, Jesus describes the Spirit as similar to wind (John 3:8) and not visible to physical eyes (John 6:46). The tenet of faith that God is Creator of all that exists involves believing that God was fully God as spirit, a nonmaterial entity, before anything material existed.

Jesus describes God as being exclusively and infinitely sovereign. God is sovereign in the kingdom of heaven (Matt. 7:21) and in the world of nature (Matt. 5:45, 6:26-32). In Luke 6:35, Jesus describes the Father as Most High, which is a superlative without equal. The synoptic Gospels record Jesus as saying that "all things are possible with God" (Matt. 19:26, Mark 10:27, Luke 18:27).

There is no more important truth about God than the quality of God's character. Jesus describes the Father as good (Mark 10:18, Luke 18:19) and as kind and merciful (Luke 6:35-36).

The most prominent characteristic of God described in the New Testament is that God is loving, as in the statement that "God is love" (1 John 4:8). The gospel of John has the most recorded statements by Jesus about love as a characteristic of God (see 13:1, 14:21-23, 15:9-10). In the Synoptics, Jesus encourages his followers to love God and one another (Matt. 22:37-39, Mark 12:30-31). In Matthew 5:44-45 and Luke 6:35-36, Jesus tells his disciples to follow the example of the Father and love even their enemies.

> The dynamic of God's love is made more graphic by noting that the words translated "love" in all the passages cited are forms of the verb *agapao* (to love because moved by esteem and care). The verb *phileo* (to love because of the emotion of friendship) is often used as a synonym. G. Abbot-Smith describes an important difference in focus.[2] *Agape* (love, care about) is a

chosen attitude based on the esteem and worth in which a person or object is held. *Philia* (love, like) is a feeling of natural affection that comes from the emotional pleasantness of association.

Agape is outwardly focused and "cares about," because a person is so highly valued. *Philia* is inwardly focused and "liked," because a person is a pleasant individual to be friends with. This distinction means that God's love is focused on persons, not on God's self, because God values persons so highly and counts persons of such great worth—even though we may not always be very likable.

Jesus reveals some distinctives about God's relation to us as human persons, for example: Jesus affirms that in creation God designed human persons as male and female, with marriage as an established relationship for reproduction and continuation of the species (Mark 10:6-9). God makes benevolent provision for human sustenance through natural law (Luke 12:22-32), because we "are of more value than many sparrows" (Luke 12:6-7).

In a metaphorical passage, Jesus says that "… my Father gives you the true bread from heaven, … that which comes down from heaven and gives life to the world" (John 6:32-33). This figurative reference is to the incarnation of Jesus who brought light and truth that nurtures the spirits of those who believe and trust. Jesus also says that God the Father and God the Son are actively present with human persons, leading, guiding, and helping in ongoing life and work (Luke 17:21, John 5:17).

When speaking of the patriarchs, Jesus says that God "is God not of the dead, but of the living" (Mark 12:27, Luke 20:38). In this affirmation, Jesus makes a distinction between the physical and spiritual features of human personhood. Although human bodies die, Jesus affirms that human persons have a spiritual self, a soul, that does not die.

God esteems human persons highly. In addition to providing generously for physical life, Jesus affirms that God desires the kind of harmony in relationship with us in which God can freely give "the Holy Spirit" and "the kingdom" to those who are "of his flock" and "who ask him" (Luke 11:13, 12:32). This aspiration of God is reflected in a familiar statement of the purpose of God in the incarnation: that "God did not send the Son into the world to condemn the world, but in order that the world might be saved through him" (John 3:17).

Learning from Jesus about Ourselves

Jesus appears to use more second-person language (person-to-person conversational teaching) than any other individual recorded in the Bible. Much of the text of the Bible is written in third person (about someone or something). Jesus often uses first person: "I say unto you." Much of his teaching is in second-person imperative, such as "come," "go," "believe," "tell," "love." As we try to understand his meaning, it is important to ask if he is informing or commanding or encouraging or prohibiting.

These are important considerations when we compare/contrast the teachings of Jesus with tenets of faith set forth by other spokespersons of religion, both biblical and unbiblical. A primary example of this is found in teachings about "choice and free will" in contrast to "election and predestination." Jesus is recorded as saying, "Repent and believe" (Mark 1:15, Matt. 4:17); "Follow me" (Matt. 4:19, Luke 5:27); "… believe in the light …" (John 12:36).

Jesus does not say whether his hearers are able to do these things. He always relates to people, instructs them, and exhorts them as though they are fully able to understand his instructions, choose whether to believe and trust what he says, and act on the basis of their choice.

Jesus describes human persons as having both physical and spiritual natures. We must have bread and water to sustain our physical body (John 4:7-14). People also need what Jesus calls "living water" that "wells up to eternal life" (v. 14), and "the bread of life" that "a man may eat of it and not die" (John 6:11, 48-50).

Jesus describes people as being of different types of character. Some walk "in the darkness" and know not "where [they] are going," while others "believe in the light" and become "children of light" (John 12:35-36). Those who "follow Jesus" and walk in the light are described as "salt of the earth" and "the light of the world" (Matt. 5:13-14). Jesus says the difference in character results from response to him as Son from the Father (John 5:23b-24).

The Gospels contain three basic tenets of faith widely held and clearly reflected in the actions and teachings of Jesus about human persons: These tenets reveal that we are loved, we are sinful, and we are worth saving.

The verse, "God so loved the world…" (John 3:16), is probably the most familiar statement from the Bible. It seems textually correct that this is not a quotation from Jesus, but commentary by the writer. The conversation with Nicodemus is first person. At verse 13 the tense shifts to third person, as explanatory commentary. However, the truth declared is clearly reflected in everything Jesus said and did.

As Jesus moves among people in his ministry, his disposition is always compassionate and his actions are kind and helpful; he "cares about" people. While his primary focus is on teaching (see Mark 1:35-39, 10:1; Matt. 4:23, 9:35; John 8:2), whenever he meets human need he turns aside to respond with gracious help (see Mark 1:29-34, Luke 13:10-12).

Jesus teaches that the Creator God cares even for animals (Matt. 6:26, 12:11), but he says clearly that people are valued more (Matt. 10:31, 12:12; Luke 12:7).

In the "I AM" discourse about the good shepherd, Jesus describes himself as "laying down" (devoting, investing, dying) his life for his sheep (John 10:11). In the last evening records, John writes of Jesus that "…having loved his own … he loved them to the end" (John 13:1).

But these "people creatures" that God cares about are sinful. Sinfulness involves both the moral/immoral features of character and the saved/lost spiritual relationship to God. Jesus does not relate to people as though they are "fated from Adam by original sin." Jesus deals with people as though they are able to make moral and spiritual choices, and as though they have made choices in life that have caused them to be alienated from harmony with God. Central to the preaching of Jesus is the admonition to repent (Matt. 4:17, Mark 1:15). Jesus proclaims that "without repentance" his hearers "will perish" (Luke 13:3, 5).

Being sinful means having chosen "to not trust instead of trust" (John 5:39-40), "disobey instead of obey" (John 3:19-20), "follow self-centeredness instead of seek harmony with" (Matt. 6:2, 5, 16; 5:20). These attitudes and actions in one's personal values and life are expressed in one's attitude toward and relationship with God. As the result of sinfulness, a person is out of sync—out of harmony—with God.

These "people creatures" whom God cares about, but who are sinful, are worth saving (Matt. 18:14). A good focus to begin this tenet of faith is with three quotations from John's gospel:

- "Men (people) loved darkness rather than light, because their deeds were evil" (3:19).
- "I have come as light into the world, so that everyone who believes in me should not remain in the darkness" (12:46).
- "I am the light of the world; whoever follows me will never walk in darkness but will have the light of life" (8:12).

Throughout, the Gospels reveal that God is loving, compassionate, caring, and forgiving, and that God takes divine initiative to seek our salvation from sinful alienation. A vital question, then, is this: How can the change from sinful alienation to reconciled harmony come to pass?

Learning from Jesus about Salvation

The tenet of soteriology (belief about salvation) evolved through the centuries. Primitive Hebrews believed the dead go to *Sheol* (the place of the dead) and "fade away" (2 Sam. 14:14, Job 10:21, Isa. 14:9-11). They had no belief in "personal survival" after physical death. By the 10th century BCE, there began to develop belief in and hope for life after death (1 Sam. 2:6, Ps. 49:15, Isa. 26:19).

Belief in salvation has a vital interrelation with belief in an afterlife beyond physical death. Is life after physical death immortality of the human spirit or resurrection life? First, some background: The Hebrew word *nephesh*

Learning from the Life and Teachings of Jesus

describes the "breath of life" in physical animals and in human persons (Gen. 1:21, 2:7). The Hebrew word *ruach* describes the Spirit of God (Ps. 51:11), and the human spirit, the "soul," the feature of human personhood that is "created in the image of God" (Gen. 1:26-27; Exod. 35:21; Ezra 1:1, 5; Ezek. 36:26-27).

The Greek language also has words that describe "living being" and "personal spirit." Paul calls the difference *psychikos* (natural man, unspiritual) and *pneumatikos* (spiritual man) (1 Cor. 2:14-15). Norman Snaith writes that there is no Old Testament reference to "soul" as surviving death. He further writes that biblical teaching is not "immortality of the human soul," but "resurrection life for those who have the Spirit and are 'in Christ'."[3] Snaith leaves us with an unresolved problem.

Non-survival of the "breath of life" feature of the physical body is not a problem, for the body is mortal and "returns to dust." If, on the other hand, the personal spirit (human soul) does not survive physical death, what is the meaning of "resurrection life"? Is resurrection life a new creation? If the soul awaits after physical death in some undefined state until the "resurrection of the body" in some eschatological future time, the soul has indeed survived death, and consequently is not mortal.

As a self-identified, nontraditional theologian, I believe that God is Spirit (John 4:24), fully and infinitely divine, without need of material body ever—past, present, or future. Therefore, I "conclude by reason" that a "resurrection body" for human persons is a metaphorical anthropomorphism describing the assured hope that a person's living soul survives physical death. Jesus "survived" his crucifixion and "presented himself alive after his passion..." (Acts 1:3).

In time, and for eternity, therefore, no concern is more vital for human persons than this question: How can the disharmony and alienation resulting from human sinfulness be made right so that harmony and reconciliation can become the relationship between God and people? In other words, how can a person "be saved"?

There are two streams of "salvation faith" in the New Testament. One stream is set forth in the Gospels, which focus on the life and teachings of Jesus. Their story is that of incarnation. In the Gospels, the evidence we have for understanding "salvation" is based on what Jesus said and did and on the remembered responses of the people.

To confirm what Jesus said about his mission as he lived and taught, consider these recorded statements from the Gospels:

- "I have come down from heaven, ... to do... the will of him who sent me" (John 6:38).
- "The Son of Man came to seek out and to save the lost" (Luke 19:10).

- "I have come ... to call ... not the righteous ... but sinners (to repentance)" (Matt. 9:13, Mark 2:17, Luke 5:31).
- "I have come as light into the world, so that everyone who believes in me should not remain in the darkness" (John 12:46).
- "Let us go on to the neighboring towns, so that I may proclaim the message there also; or that is what I came out to do (Mark 1:38),
- "... for I was sent for this purpose" (Luke 4:43).

Also, consider these statements from Jesus about how alienated sinners are reconciled to harmony with God:

- "... the kingdom of God has come near; repent, and believe in the good news" (Mark 1:14-15, see also Matt. 4:17).
- "...I said unto you, 'You must be born from above,'" for "... "no one can see (or enter) the kingdom of God without being born from above (John 3:7, 3).
- "Anyone who hears my word and believes him who sent me has eternal life ... (and) has passed from death to life" (John 5:24).
- "Whoever follows me will never walk in darkness but will have the light of life" (John 8:12).

(I do not include John 3:16 among these citations because the evidence convinces me that the change to third person at verse 13 means that John 3:13-21 is commentary by the writer, not a direct quote from Jesus. I clearly affirm that I believe as absolute truth that "... everyone who believes in him may not perish but may have eternal life.")

Jesus is not recorded to have set forth any transactional ritual by which a person is given a status of "being saved." Rather, as confirmed in the following passages, Jesus taught about believing truths in harmony with the character of God, standards of human character and conduct that are in sync with the character of God, and ways of trust and life by which a transformed relationship (a new spiritual birth from above) becomes a reality for a person.

- "Not everyone who says to me, 'Lord, Lord,' will enter the kingdom of heaven, but only the one who does the will of my Father in heaven" (Matt. 7:21).
- "This is indeed the will of my Father, that all who see the Son and believe in him may have eternal life" (John 6:40).
- "... it is not the will of your Father in heaven that one of these little ones should be lost" (Matt. 18:14).

Learning from the Life and Teachings of Jesus

Matthew and Mark record two central teachings by Jesus: "the kingdom of God/heaven is at hand" and his hearers are called "to repent" (Matt. 4:17, Mark 1:15). Mark adds that "time is fulfilled" and people are called "to believe the gospel." Jesus teaches that the beneficent sovereignty of God is in effect here and now. The status of people in relationship to God is determined by whether the values in what they believe and how they live are in harmony with the character and sovereignty of God. The central feature of repentant faith is vital to a tenet of salvation based on the teachings of Jesus.

The synoptic Gospels focus on Jesus' teachings regarding how to live in harmony with God. Traits of character and conduct called the Beatitudes are set at the beginning of the Sermon on the Mount (Matt. 5:3-11). Jesus gives clear instructions about what to do and what not to do. Luke records some of these same teachings (Luke 6:20-38). Jesus says, "Love your enemies, and do good and .... your reward will be great, and you will be sons/children of the Most High" (Luke 6:35).

It seems evident that Jesus believes people are capable of doing what he teaches, and freely competent to choose whether or not to do it. In the parables of the kingdom, Jesus describes the beginning as a seed sown or a bit of yeast tucked into dough (Matt. 13:31-33, Mark 4:30-32, Luke 13:18-21). There is no great ceremony of citizenship bestowal, but the beginning of a "new life" that in turn becomes a "growth in grace."

A critical key for entering the kingdom, however, is that it must be so desired and valued that it is like a "pearl of great value" or a "treasure hidden in a field" for which the finder "gives all to possess" (Matt. 13:44-46). Jesus does not set forth rituals to be done, but simply describes choices of value to be lived: "Go and learn what this means, 'I desire mercy, not sacrifice'" (Matt. 9:13); "... unless your righteousness exceeds that of the scribes and Pharisees, you will never enter the kingdom of heaven" (Matt. 5:20). (The Greek word translated "shall exceed" in the King James Version means either "exceed in number" or "excel in value by being of a better kind." "Excel" is better in this context.)[4]

The Fourth Gospel also records statements by Jesus about reconciliation between sinful humanity and God. I am convinced, however, that two features of John's gospel are crucially important for understanding this gospel: the focus on "signs" (the physical phenomena that reveal Jesus as the incarnate Son of God) and the writer's widespread use of metaphors (figurative expressions to describe spiritual truths and relationship conditions).

Metaphor examples are found in the "I AM sayings" in John, where Jesus describes himself as the:

- "bread of life" (6:35)
- "light of the world" (8:12)
- "gate for the sheep" (10:7)
- "good shepherd" (10:11)
- "resurrection and the life" (11:25)
- "way, the truth, and the life" (14:6)
- "vine" (15:5)

John also includes metaphor examples to describe relationships:

- "I am the living bread" ... "whoever eats of this bread will live forever" ... "the bread that I will give for the life of the world is my flesh" (6:51).
- "Unless you eat the flesh of the Son of Man and drink his blood, you have no life in you" (6:53).

(If understood as literal, Jesus would be describing cannibalism, which is certainly untenable. It seems evident that Jesus uses "flesh" to mean "incarnation," and "blood" to mean "life.")

I understand this teaching by Jesus to mean that "believing in Jesus as one come from God to bring 'light for life'" and "trusting the teachings of Jesus as he 'gave' (invested) his life in ministry" are the human responses that lead to a "new birth in spirit from above" and, in turn, harmony with God and eternal life (see John 10:27-30).

In summary, the teachings of Jesus set forth an experience of transformational human conversion. God offers love, grace, and forgiveness. A person believes the good news enough to turn to God in repentant faith and trusting commitment. Reconciliation and harmony become real, and a believer experiences a new birth in spirit from God. This is a spiritual event involving the Holy Spirit of the Sovereign God and the personal spirit/soul of a human person who becomes a new creature in Christ. Jesus does not teach about any ritual involved as a transaction in the transformation.

The other stream of "salvation faith" set forth in the New Testament is the doctrine based on Paul's writing about justification being necessary to erase sinful guilt, and justice being satisfied by the substitutionary sacrifice of Jesus in crucifixion. That discussion belongs in the development of doctrines among early Christians after the Incarnation. Later, a group of Christian rituals, beginning with baptism and Eucharist (Lord's Supper), are elevated by the church fathers to have sacrament-producing effect.

Learning from Jesus about Eternity

The subject of end times and eternity brings us to the most difficult tenets of faith to comprehend and to organize. The different concepts are very complex and varied. Much about everything beyond physical death is merely speculation. Not even all that is recorded to have been said by Jesus can be reconciled as consistent. Many of the images that have become fixed in traditional beliefs about "end times" do not have reliable foundation. Nevertheless, the developed traditions that the gospel writers recorded from a

> long generation or two after the life and times of Jesus do include passages about the relationship of and difference between "time" and "eternity."
> The most widely used reference to this subject in the Gospels is the phrase "kingdom of God/heaven." Context must guide in trying to understand "now" or "then." The most crucial difference for trying to understand this is a person's belief about the relationship of and the difference between the material and the nonmaterial, the physical and the spiritual. The spiritual aspect must always be kept primary and priority, which is difficult for us because we live in a physical world that is inescapably real for us until our bodies die in physical death.

Jesus uses the phrase "kingdom of God/heaven" to describe the kingdom as having "come near" (Matt. 4:17; Mark 1:15; Luke 10:9, 11), having "come to you" (Matt. 12:28, Luke 11:20), is "among you" or "within" you (Luke 17:21). His reference seems surely to mean present time, not future beyond time. I believe Jesus is describing a relationship in human life, in present time, in which the sovereignty of God is accepted as prevailing and is embraced by trust. This relationship becomes real through God's forgiving grace, and a sinful person's repentant faith and new birth from above. A person becomes "a child of the King."

It is equally clear that Jesus talks about a world beyond this world, a realm of spirit different than the material universe in which we physically live. God is unquestionably sovereign in both worlds. The "end time" questions for us are the fate of the physical universe, and the nature of human existence after physical death—if there is indeed an afterlife.

We cannot understand the biblical records in regard to these questions without starting with a perspective on one of our basic human problems. We simply do not have concepts, categories for comparison, nor adequate language to describe and explain spiritual realities. Consider these figurative metaphors about spiritual realities:

- Language in the Gospels about "life in the realm beyond" includes many material images: thrones and seats beside them (Matt. 20:20-21, Mark 10:35-37, Luke 22:28-30), tables and feasts on them (Matt. 8:11-12, Luke 13:29).

- The records of statements by Jesus about "end times" and "afterlife" are largely just references without explanatory information: "that day," "day of judgment," and "end of the age" (Matt. 7:22, 10:15, 13:39-49).

- There are references to celebratory events: "eat bread in the kingdom of heaven" and "sit on seats beside the throne" (Matt. 20:22-23, Mark 10:40).

- There are references to punitive suffering: "be liable to the hell of fire," "be cast into hell" (Matt. 5:22-30, 10:28; Mark 9:44-46).

- The most descriptive statements by Jesus refer to consequences in the "afterlife" for conduct in this life: "give an account for every careless word you utter" (Matt. 12:36); "as you did it" or "as you did not do it" (Matt. 25:31-46); "those who have done good … those who have done evil" (John 5:29).

- There are also passages that are end-time/apocalyptic in nature (Matt. 24:3-31; Mark 13:1-7, 14-27; Luke 17:20-37, 21:5-28). Three features are comingled in these passages: the coming destruction of Jerusalem and the Temple, the "coming" of Jesus, and the end of the world.

The parallel passages in the synoptic Gospels cannot be understood without awareness about the "day of the Lord" proclamations and tenets of faith that developed in Israel/Judah in the 8th century and following:

- Amos in Israel and Isaiah in Judah (8th century BCE) first proclaimed a coming "day" in which the Lord will show his sovereignty and punish the waywardness of Israel (Amos 5:18-20, 8:9-10; Isa. 2:6-12, 20-21).
- The prophets heralded hope for the restoration of national Israel and promised doom for the oppressing adversaries (Jer. 46:10, Ezek. 30:3-5). Does the resolving come about by satisfying the just demands of God that appropriate penalty be paid for guilt before forgiveness will be granted?
- The postexilic prophets continue the message of the "day of the Lord" (Joel 2:1-2, 30-31, 3:14-16; Obad. 15; Zeph. 1:14-18).

The biblical prophets focused their message about the "day of the Lord" on then-current situations, and themes of sovereignty and judgment, of hoped-for reward and reckoning. During the inter-biblical period, the "day of the Lord" tenets of faith developed into end-time apocalyptic faiths and figures (Daniel 7–12 and Apocryphal writings).[5]

I share with many interpreters that the passages recorded as statements by Jesus are troublesome to me. The passages are very kindred with writings in Jewish apocalyptic literature from the troubled times of Greek empire end, centuries of Palestine disorder and conflict, and Maccabean revolt, before Roman dominance after 67 BCE. All of the statements by Jesus about the "coming of the Son of Man" are found in these apocalyptic end-time passages, with accompanying images of persecution, tribulation, and natural cataclysms.

The Gospels themselves were written in a time of Roman persecution of Christians, of national turmoil leading up to the Jewish revolt in 64 CE, which led to the Roman sack of Jerusalem and destruction of the Temple in 70 CE. These passages describe events, and beliefs about them, that are not present in the teachings of Jesus before Passion Week. Before that time, even the disciples have not been able to grasp what Jesus is talking about when he speaks of his death (Mark 9:32; Luke 9:45, 18:34).

Jewish religion in general, and end-time hopes in particular, are different in focus from the life example and teachings of Jesus. A central focus of post-kingdom Judaism is upon events and the transactions that result from them (Isa. 5:8-13; Amos 2:6-8, 13-16; Joel 1:13-15). Jesus exemplifies by life, and sets forth in teaching, the importance of relationships and the qualities of character that build harmony in relationships (Matt. 18:15-22; Luke 6:27-36; John 12:44-46, 14:23).

There is wide divergence among interpreters about Jesus and "end time" beliefs. We have no evidence-based certainty about the subject. I personally find apocalyptic writings "out of character" when compared to the teachings of Jesus. I cannot conclude but that the passages as we have them in the Gospels are additions to the traditions before the texts were written. Jesus teaches about how we become "people of God" during our physical lives. What we become, through faith and grace in relation to God, has consequences for "what we are" in the realm of spirit beyond physical death.

***

The crucifixion brought an end to the incarnate physical life and teachings of Jesus. His followers were devastated. They were not expecting a resurrection. When Jesus "… presented himself alive …" (Acts 1:3), their hopes were restored. Everything changed for them. Much of their former Jewish religion no longer had the same meaning. The Jewish Torah was still sacred to them, but they had no "Christian" scriptures to guide them. They were now the first "people of the way." It was for them to begin a new movement in religion, to give rise to new tenets of faith based on their memories from Jesus and inspiration by the Holy Spirit of God. Their story, which began on Easter morning, developed through four centuries before the New Testament was canonized. The beginnings of the Christian faith is the story of the first Christian centuries.

Notes

[1] Marcus J. Borg and John Dominic Crossan, *The Last Week* (San Francisco: Harper Collins, 2006), 7-8.

[2] G. Abbott-Smith, *Manual Greek Lexicon of the New Testament*, 3rd ed. (Edinburgh: T&T Clark, 1950), 3-4, 469-470.

[3] Norman H. Snaith, "The Language of the Old Testament," *The Interpreter's Bible*, vol. 1 (New York: Abingdon Press, 1952), 230b.

[4] Abbot-Smith, *Lexicon*, 357

[5] Robert H. Pfeiffer, "Apocalypses," *The Interpreter's Bible*, vol. 1 (New York: Abingdon Press, 1952), 427-432.

Chapter 6
Learning from Acts and the Pauline Letters

The New Testament books record the early development of the tenets of the Christian faith. These documents, though not placed in chronological order, fall into three groups: the Gospels, Acts and the letters of Paul, and the post-Pauline documents.

> The Gospels (written in 64/5–100 CE) are based on four streams of tradition that developed from eyewitness memories and the telling and retelling of those stories for one or two long generations. Matthew is the only gospel believed to have developed in the Jewish world around Jerusalem. Mark is believed to have come from Simon Peter's witness from prison in Rome. Luke reflects the Gentile world of Paul and Luke, with later research by Luke and information from Mark. John is the least historically oriented and is believed to have been crafted as a theological document in the Ephesus area of Asia Minor.

Having already examined the life and teachings of Jesus as recorded in the Gospels, we will now follow the chronological sequence of Acts and the Pauline letters.

Acts and the letters of Paul (written in 50-65 CE) are treasured among the churches and place a "Pauline stamp" on the developing stream of faith. The title "Acts of the Apostles" is only partially accurate, as it covers the first period accounts of the apostles and the disciple group until the conversion of Saul/Paul. After Paul's conversion, Acts becomes the Pauline story. The religious beliefs in the biblical texts after the Gospels are tenets of faith that develop within the Christian movement. Written during the first century after the death of Jesus, they are finally canonized into the New Testament nearly three centuries later.

The tenets of the Christian faith begin with the followers of Jesus, numbering about 120 (Acts 1:15). With Jesus no longer physically present to lead them, his followers will have to make fundamental decisions about what life going forward will mean for them. Are they to go back to their earlier ways of life, as Simon Peter appears to be considering (John 21:3)?

From the beginning, the apostles (eleven, without Judas) are considered to be the leaders of the group. Acts does not describe them as continuing to cower in fear for their lives. Led by Simon Peter, they replace Judas with Matthias. First-person association with Jesus in the years of his incarnate ministry is considered vital for being added to the group of eleven (Acts 1:21-26).

Jesus had promised the presence of the Holy Spirit to abide, lead, and enable the apostles after his death (John 14:15-26). The disciples needed the resurrection appearances to renew and confirm their assurance that Jesus is alive. The larger group needs the Pentecost event to assure them that the Holy Spirit is indeed present with and enabling them for the ministry Jesus had commissioned them to do (Acts 2:1-11).

At the beginning, the group has no authority to which they can appeal: the Hebrew scriptures are their only sacred writings. The "followers of the way" are dependent on their earlier religious experiences in Judaism, their memories from life with Jesus, and the inspiration of the Holy Spirit. For them, it is now time to respond to their sense of purpose to which Jesus has sent them into the world (John 17:18).

The apostles spend time in the Temple "praising and blessing God" (Luke 24:52-53 KJV), which results in conflicts with the Temple leadership (Acts 4:1-22). Records in the Bible do not detail the way Christians become separated from all Jewish activities in the Temple and synagogues, but other sources describe the division as gradual and differing in time from place to place. The first recorded public proclamations are as follow:

- Peter's sermon at Pentecost (Acts 2:14-36)
- Peter and John's sermon before the people and their defense before the Sanhedrin (Acts 3:11–4:12)
- Stephen's defense before his death (Acts 6:8–7:53)
- Philip's witness to the Ethiopian (Acts 8:27-39)

The apostles' presentations are based on review of Jewish national and religious heritage, leading up to declarations about Jesus and his death, resurrection, and exaltation.

The apostles base their faith in Jesus on the traditional Jewish messianic hope for a "king in David's dynastic line redeeming (restoring) national Israel" (Luke 24:21; Acts 1:6, 2:36, 3:18, 8:5). Included in their preaching are features of different beliefs about the Messiah:

- Messiah will be a "son of David" (Acts 2:29-30).
- Messiah will be a "suffering servant" (Acts 2:23, 4:24-26, 8:32-35).
- Messiah has triumphed over death through resurrection (Acts 2:31-32, 4:10, 7:56).
- Messiah's reign is now to be in a future "established time" (Acts 3:20-21).

The title Messiah/Christ (the Anointed One) is joined with the name Jesus (Jehovah saves) to become a two-word personal name, Jesus Christ, in Christian usage. With messianic hope being cast into the future through the Resurrection, focus shifts from a mission to "redeem Israel" to a mission of "salvation from sinfulness" (Acts 4:12).

After the stoning of Stephen and the introduction of Saul/Paul, a scattering of the "church" follows (Acts 7:54–8:3). The scattered disciples continue their witnessing and ministry (Acts 8:4). Repentance and baptism become associated with faith, forgiveness, and conversion (Acts 2:38, 8:35-38). Laying on hands becomes a ritual associated with setting apart for service and receiving the Holy Spirit (Acts 6:6, 8:14-17).

Simon Peter has an experience with Cornelius that God uses to persuade Peter that "what God has made clean, you must not call profane" (Acts 11:9). Peter says, "If then God gave them (Gentiles) the same gift (Holy Spirit) that he gave us (Jews) when we believed in the Lord Jesus Christ, who was I that I could withstand God?" (Acts.11:17). The apostles then agree and praise God that "repentance that leads to life" is granted to Gentiles along with Jews (Acts 11:18).

This acceptance of Gentile inclusion by Christians is the first major change in religious belief after the resurrection of Jesus and the manifestation of the Holy Spirit at Pentecost. The next major change comes with the conversion of Saul of Tarsus.

The Conversion and Inclusion of Paul

Saul first appears as a violent adversary of the Christians. He is present at and approves of the stoning of Stephen (Acts 7:59–8:1), becoming a zealous persecutor of Christians (Acts 9:1-2). On the way to Damascus, Saul is smitten with guilt in an overwhelming experience with Jesus. His guilt drives him into submission, conversion, and total redirection of his life (Acts 9:3-6). In Damascus he is regarded with suspicion, but a believer named Ananias is inspired to believe Saul's conversion. Once accepted into the group of believers, Saul witnesses among them and in the synagogues about Jesus as Messiah (Acts 9:19-22).

The Jews then become Saul's adversary, just as Saul was before an adversary of Christians. The Jews plot to kill him. Saul has to leave Damascus and return to Jerusalem (Acts 9:23-25), where he is well-known and feared. Barnabas believes Saul's account of conversion and "sponsors" his acceptance into the believer group (Acts 9:26-28).

There has already developed some sense of separateness between Jewish-culture Christians and Greek-culture Christians (Acts 6:1). The Hellenists (Grecians, Greek-culture Christians) violently oppose Saul, and seek to kill him, causing division in the group. The leaders take Saul to the port city of Caesarea and send him home to Tarsus (Acts 9:30). A period of peace results (Acts 9:31).

The scattering that results from the persecution led by Saul results in Christian groups developing in the northern Mediterranean coastal area, the island of Cyprus, and the city of Antioch—all in non-Jewish territory (Acts 11:19). In Antioch the question of Gentile acceptance into Christianity arises (Acts 11:19-22). The church (which has become the identifying name of the Christian groups) in Jerusalem sends Barnabas to Antioch to check into the matter.

The full acceptance of Gentiles is not fully established for some years, and never accepted by the Judaizers. When Barnabas observes the grace of God in the lives of Gentile Christians, he affirms it and brings Saul back from Tarsus for active ministry in Antioch (Acts 11:23-26). A time of peace and growth prevails.

The Missionary Spread of Christianity

The Christian gospel is first taken outside of Jewish territory because of persecution that drives some of the believers away from Jerusalem (Acts 11:19). Soon, the missionary spirit manifests itself. Barnabas and Saul are set apart by laying on hands, and "the mission" begins (Acts. 13:2-3).

Barnabas and Saul, along with John Mark, go first to the island of Cyprus. There, at Paphos, the name of Saul changes to Paul. After leaving Cyprus, they go into the Gentile territory of central Asia Minor where they preach in synagogues. The Jew/Gentile problem arises, and they are driven from place to place. After preaching in four cities, they retrace their path and return to Antioch in Phoenicia (Acts 13:4–14:28).

No distinctive new religious beliefs are described on this missionary journey, but in his sermon at Antioch of Pisidia, Paul declares, "… that through this man (Jesus) forgiveness of sins is proclaimed to you; by this Jesus everyone who believes is set free from all those sins from which you could not be freed by the law of Moses" (Acts 13:38-39). Paul makes no mention of any ritual or substitute sacrifice involved in receiving forgiveness.

The unresolved matter of Gentile acceptance into the Christian faith arises again (Acts 13:44-50, 14:1-2). Paul, Barnabas, and some others are sent to Jerusalem to "discuss this question with the apostles and elders" (Acts 15:2). After debate, Simon Peter becomes a vital witness about his experience with Cornelius (Acts 10). Barnabas and Paul give witness of their experience. James, the brother of Jesus and a recognized leader in the Jerusalem church, then speaks (Acts 15:13).

James suggests a compromise: The Jews will fully accept Gentile Christians. In turn, the Gentile Christians will show consideration of Jewish sensitivities by abstaining from idolatry, unchastity, and consuming blood (Acts 15:19-21). The compromise becomes the established practice (Acts 15:22-29), but the controversy does not go away.

Paul and Barnabas agree to begin a second journey. They disagree about John Mark going with them, however, so they separate. Barnabas takes Mark and goes to Cyprus, and is not heard from again except in Paul's later references to him (Acts 15:36-39). Paul takes Silas, and they travel through Syria (the Roman name for Phoenicia) and Cilicia (the region around Tarsus, Paul's native home). They visit the churches begun on the first journey. At Lystra, Timothy joins them (Acts 16:1-3). They continue west to Troas (ancient Troy of the Trojan Wars) on the coast of the Aegean Sea. There, Paul experiences the "Macedonian vision" and they go over to Philippi (Acts 16:10). Apparently, Luke joins the group at Troas (Acts 16:8, 10).

> This is a significant move for the four men, for it takes them from Asia Minor to Greece. It is not a radical move, however, because both provinces are Roman territory. But in modern times it has been considered very important because it is a move from Asia to Europe, allowing Christianity to develop as a western religion in Europe and North America

Paul continues his practice of seeking out Jewish groups to "evangelize" first. He encounters the Gentile Christian problem, as he did in Asia Minor, and in Greece he begins to be opposed by Roman culture and Greek religions (Acts 16:16-23).

Paul and Silas are imprisoned, and while in prison two significant things happen: The prison is breached by an earthquake, but Paul refuses to escape and persuades the jailer to not commit suicide. (Apparently, the jailer expects the prisoners to flee, and his life would be exacted for nonperformance of duty.) He asks Paul, "What must I do to be saved (rescued from this peril to my life)?" Paul makes it an opportunity for Christian witness, and the jailer's household is led to faith and baptized.

The next morning the magistrates send for Paul and Silas to be released. Paul challenges them for public abuse and claims his privilege as a Roman citizen, leading the officials to apologize and personally release him and Silas (Acts 16:35-39).

From Philippi, Paul and Silas travel down the eastern coast of Greece to Thessalonica and Berea. At Thessalonica, Paul includes in his preaching "that it was necessary for the Messiah to suffer and to rise from the dead" (Acts 17:3). This statement indicates that Paul has fully transitioned from having the "messianic hope of a son of David restoring national Israel" to Jesus becoming "Messiah, as Isaiah's suffering servant, triumphant over death, and King of future messianic hope." After being driven out of Thessalonica and Berea, Paul arrives at Athens.

In Athens he encounters philosophers who disparage his preaching (Acts 17:16-33). Paul then leaves Athens and goes to Corinth. At Corinth he meets a Jewish couple, Aquila and Priscilla, and resides with them and joins in their craft of tentmaking (Acts 18:3). This is the first reference to Paul's trade. In his letter back to them, Paul describes himself among the "apostles, … who labor and work with our hands" (1 Cor. 4:9-12). In his second letter to the Corinthians, Paul reminds them that he took no support from them when he worked among them (2 Cor. 11:8-9). Aquila and Priscilla become Christians and long-time associates of Paul.

At Corinth, the controversy between Paul and the Jews becomes so harsh that he declares, "From now on I will go to the Gentiles" (Acts 18:6). Paul stays in Corinth a year and a half (Acts 18:11), his longest tenure with any church except Ephesus. (On his third journey he stays in Ephesus more than two years [Acts 19:8-10].)

Paul leaves Corinth to return to Jerusalem and Antioch, stopping by Ephesus and promising to come back to them "if God wills." After some time in Antioch, Paul begins his third, and last, missionary journey (Acts 18:22-23).

He travels through Asia Minor again, visiting churches along the way, but heads to Ephesus to fulfill the promise he has made. He encounters the incomplete teaching of Apollos and leads the disciples to receive the Holy Spirit. For new Christians, baptism and laying on of hands for receipt of the Holy Spirit has become an ongoing practice by Paul (Acts 19:4-6).

Paul goes first to the synagogue, but is opposed and therefore leaves to work with both Jews and Gentiles (Acts 19:8-10). Jewish exorcists lead to a controversy and the exposure of magicians. A major "book burning" takes place (Acts 19:11-19).

At Ephesus, Paul reveals a plan to visit churches in Greece, then return to Jerusalem, and finally to go to Rome (Acts 19:21-22). Though it is not recorded here, we know that Paul is gathering an "alms offering" for the needy church in Jerusalem (1 Cor. 16:1-4; 2 Cor. 8:16-22, 9:1-5; Acts 24:17). Before leaving Ephesus, Paul is accused by the silversmiths of violating the city's allegiance to Artemis and endangering their flourishing shrine-making trade. The town clerk quiets the turmoil, tells the silversmiths to go to court, and dismisses the crowd. Paul makes a last visit to the churches around the Aegean Sea, stopping by Miletus to visit the Ephesian elders before sailing to Judea (Acts 20:36-38).

Paul is warned to avoid going to Jerusalem (Acts 21:10-12). In an effort to avoid trouble, the church leaders ask him to "go through the rite of purification" and pay for four young men under vows to have their heads shaved (Acts 21:22-24). The angry Jews see Paul and Throphimus (an Ephesian Gentile) together (Acts 21:29), and they assume the two men have been in the Temple. The city is thrown into turmoil, and the residents are determined to kill Paul. The Romans move in to quell the riot, however (Acts 21: 31-33).

Paul asks, and is granted, permission to speak to the crowd. He finally has to appeal to his Roman citizenship to avoid being beaten (Acts 21:39, 22:24-29). Paul is tried before the Sanhedrin, and civil unrest follows. The Jews scheme in an ongoing effort to "get at" Paul to kill him. Their scheme is known, so plans are made to send Paul to Caesarea for trial before the Roman governor Felix (Acts 23:1-35).

Felix will not decide for Paul against the Jews and is later replaced by Festus (Acts 24). Festus wishes to use Paul's case to gain favor with the Jews. Paul takes advantage of his Roman citizenship and appeals to the emperor (Acts. 25:1-12). Paul is secured from Jewish enmity, but left in prison.

After his lengthy time in prison in Caesarea, Paul sails toward Rome, accompanied by Luke (Acts 27:2-3). The trip is long and treacherous, involving a shipwreck at Malta (Acts 27:4-44), but Paul and Luke finally arrive in Rome. Paul is greeted by the Christians there with welcome (Acts 28:15). The reaction of Jewish leaders in Rome is quite different and divided (Acts 28:14-25). Paul makes a firm proclamation about unbelieving Jews and the inclusion of Gentiles (Acts 28:25-29). Luke concludes the record in Acts with Paul imprisoned in Rome. Paul has limited confinement, living on his own, and having freedom to teach and preach (Acts 28:30-31). The final outcome of his imprisonment and appeal is unknown.

Paul's Beliefs and Influence

In the theology chapters of his letter to the Romans (1–11), Paul sets forth and applies three major tenets of the Christian faith:

- justification and grace in the character of God
- election and predestination in regards to people
- universal sin, making substitutionary sacrificial redemption necessary before salvation by faith is possible

The sources of these tenets of faith are readily identifiable in the heritage of Paul's Jewish faith, which he learned in the rabbinical school of Gamaliel (Acts 5:34, 22:3).

Justification and Grace

Paul believes that sinfulness and disobedience corrupt human persons with guilt that offends the righteousness of God (Exod. 34:7; Deut. 4:24, 6:15; Josh. 24:19-20). God's sense of justice requires that justifying penalty be paid or wrath be suffered (Rom. 1:18, Eph. 5:6, Col. 3:6). Paul, however, also belongs to the historic tradition of Jewish faith that believes God is gracious (Exod. 34:6-7, Ps. 86:15, Joel 2:13, writing that "… where sin increased, grace abounded all the more" (Rom. 5:20).

Paul believes the dilemma of justification and grace is resolved by a divine action. God "put forward" Jesus as "a sacrifice of atonement by his blood," so that sinners may be "… justified by his (God's) grace as a gift." This is, according to Paul, God's plan of salvation for sinners "… through the redemption that is in Christ Jesus" which is made "… effective through faith" (Rom. 3:24-25; 5:2, 9).

Election and Predestination

Paul's belief in election follows in the tradition of faith that God's call of Abraham established a status of "chosen people" for Abraham's descendants. Through the centuries their faith has developed from polytheism to monotheism, one universal sovereign God. Jewish belief about "chosen" status with God does not develop to include all people as God's people on equal standing. As the "apostle to the Gentiles," Paul does indeed believe that "in Christ, there is neither Jew nor Greek (Gentile), …" (Gal. 3:28). Nevertheless, Paul still describes Israel as the true "olive tree," and the Gentile Christians as "wild olive branches grafted in" (Rom. 11:17-24). He believes that "not all Israelites truly belong to Israel" (Rom. 9:6), but that "... all Israel will be saved" (Rom. 11:26).

Paul writes that election and predestination are based on foreknowledge (Rom. 8:29), and that the predestined are called and justified (Rom. 8:30). Salvation then is made effective by faith reception of the free gift of grace (Eph. 2:8). Paul writes as if he believes that the sacrificed blood of Jesus expiates the corruption of original sin from Adam's disobedience (Rom. 3:23-25, 5:9-10).

The question Paul leaves unanswered is whether election and predestination leave any freedom of response to repent, believe, have faith, and receive the grace of forgiveness and life in Christ. For instance, Paul describes some Israelites as branches broken off the native olive tree because of unbelief (Rom. 11:20). They will, "if they do not persist in unbelief," be "grafted in, ... back into their own olive tree" (Rom. 11:23-24).

According to Paul, salvation comes "by grace ... through faith" (Eph. 2:8). But the question arises: Is faith a gift from God or a responding choice by a freely-believing person? In his writing about election, Paul declares that "it depends not on human will or exertion, but on God who shows mercy" (Rom. 9:16). Since Paul is writing about people "arguing with God" about election (Rom. 9:19), it seems certain that he is using "vessels" to represent persons. In this passage Paul leaves no doubt that he believes God has every right to make "objects of wrath made for destruction" and "objects of mercy, which he has prepared beforehand for glory" (Rom. 9:22-23). These appear to be destiny-determining actions by God, not responses of believing faith by people. The dilemma remains, with no definitive answer.

Sin and Salvation

> There is no tenet of faith expressed by Paul more important than his beliefs about salvation. Paul is a primary activist in the early spread of Christianity, the writer of letters that become the earliest documents later canonized into the New Testament, and a formative influence in the beliefs that become established as the Christian message. From Paul, the tenet of blood atonement by the substitute sacrifice of Jesus in crucifixion becomes the traditional doctrine of salvation in Christian theology.

Paul believes in "original sin" and its effects upon all humanity, writing that "... by one man's disobedience the many were made sinners" (Rom. 5:19), and "...one man's trespass led to condemnation for all (mankind)" (Rom. 5:18). (This belief is based on the disobedience by Adam and Eve in the story of Eden and "humanity's fall" (Gen. 2:15-17, 3:6. See pp. 1-2, 39-40 for a discussion of the history of this biblical story in postexilic Judaism.)

Paul also writes that "… all have sinned and fall short of the glory of God " (Rom. 3:23), affirming that sinfulness is a "way of life" in the present for all people.

These beliefs are Paul's understanding of where all people begin in their relationship with God. Based on his earlier life in Judaism, Paul is steeped in Mosaic rituals and regulations. He affirms that "God has done what the law, weakened by the flesh, could not do: by sending his own Son in the likeness of sinful flesh, and to deal with sin, he condemned sin in the flesh" (Rom. 8:3). How does Paul believe the sin problem can be resolved, and how can people be saved and have harmony with God?

Paul describes a process in which election and redemption of the elect are planned by God for the "fullness of time" (Eph. 1:7-10). Paul surely agrees that God's plan for redemption of the elect is rightly described in a summary statement in 1 Peter 1:18-20, "… You were ransomed … with the precious blood of Christ, like that of a lamb without defect or blemish. He (Christ) was destined before the foundation of the world, but was revealed at the end of the ages for your sake."

The Jews believe that "without the shedding of blood there is no forgiveness of sins" (Heb. 9:22) and that "it is impossible that the blood of bulls and goats should take away sins" (Heb. 10:4). By contrast, Paul believes that the "purity of his (Jesus') blood" and the "perfection of his sacrifice" is sufficient "once for all at the end of the age to remove sin by the sacrifice of himself" (Heb. 9:26). His belief in this predestined process of redemption is based on his belief in justification, namely, that God is a God of justice. Furthermore, Paul believes that:

- Justice requires that an adequate penalty must be paid to justify the cleansing (expiation) of sinful guilt from Adam's original sin before forgiveness can be granted.
- God in grace chose "before the foundation of the world" to provide the justifying penalty to make justified forgiveness possible. Since the blood of animals is not sufficient, God predestined the pure divine blood to be shed in substitute sacrifice to expiate the corrupting guilt of original sin.
- Since God by grace has justified sinners by the blood of Jesus, God's gift of forgiving grace is now available to be received by justified and forgiven sinners by faith (Rom. 3:24-25).

Paul believes that "salvation from sin" becomes effective for those who receive God's gracious free gift of redeeming forgiveness by faith (Eph. 2:4-8). He describes the effect of the experience of salvation as "the Spirit of God dwells in you" (Rom. 8:9); being "in Christ, there is a new creation" (2 Cor. 5:17); having your life "hidden with Christ in God" (Col. 3:3). Paul describes the Christian life after salvation in ways that are in harmony with the teachings of Jesus.

How Paul Differs from Jesus

> There is an absence in the teaching of Jesus about some tenets that are central to Paul's beliefs. I find no record that Jesus ever referred to the Garden of Eden, the "fall of man," or original sin/universal guilt/fated perdition. Evidence is convincing that these tenets were first brought into Jewish faith during the Babylonian Exile, but Jesus does not base any teaching on them. Jesus is also not recorded to have given any teaching on the necessity of justifying sacrifice to expiate the guilt of inherited sin from parents or from an original corrupting source. Jesus is forthright in considering sinfulness a common, even universal, human condition. Jesus seems clearly, however, to deal with sinfulness as a current moral and spiritual condition resulting from personal life values that result in disharmony and an out-of-sync relationship with God. Jesus teaches that reconciliation with God comes through repentant change of life values, trusting faith in God, and commitment of life following a new birth of spirit.

Paul's development of the Christian faith is important for several reasons:

- Paul evidently neither sees nor hears Jesus teach, although he is in Jerusalem while Jesus is living and teaching.
- Paul self-identifies as having been a Pharisaic Jew, reared in Jerusalem and educated in the rabbinical school of Gamaliel (Acts 22:3, 5:34; Phil. 3:4-6).
- Paul seems to have never learned about the life and teachings of Jesus from any of the eyewitnesses of Jesus (Acts 9:26-30; Gal. 1:13-23; 2 Cor. 11:5, 12:11).
- Paul does not cite the teachings of Jesus as the basis for his beliefs and practices, but bases his Christian beliefs on what he understands as direct personal revelations on the road to Damascus and throughout his ministry (Acts 9:4-6; 1 Cor. 2:7-10; Eph. 1:9, 3:3).
- Paul's Jewish heritage appears to be reflected in his preference of the name "Christ Jesus" rather than "Jesus Christ," giving emphasis to the messianic role of Jesus.

The Inclusion of Gentiles

Paul believes that the inclusion of Gentiles has been a part of God's plan for ages, and describes the process by which God brings it about. First, some of elect Israel is broken off the "olive tree" because of their unbelief (Rom. 11:20). Gentiles, branches of wild olive trees, are grafted in who "stand fast only through faith." Paul writes that the salvation of Gentiles will "make Israel jealous" (Rom. 11:11), and "if they (Jewish branches) do not persist in unbelief" they will be grafted in again (Rom. 11:23, 30-31) so "all Israel will be saved" (Rom. 11:26). Both Gentiles and Jews are included in the benefits of the justifying sacrifice of Jesus' crucifixion, ... "you were bought with a price" (1 Cor. 6:20, 7:23).

Paul describes himself as "an apostle to the Gentiles" (Rom. 11:13), on the basis of personal revelation from God that the "inclusion" of the Gentiles is part of the mystery of God, hidden through the ages (Eph. 1:9-10, 2:11-22), so "all of you are one in Christ Jesus" (Gal. 3:28).

The Christian Life

Paul's writings about the Christian life raise again the question about whether or not a person has free will. He writes about the transformed life that befits a Christian, but in his description of his own personal struggle he describes an inability to live a transformed life. He speaks of being liberated from "slavery to sin" and becoming "slaves of righteousness" (Rom.6:16-18), and in the present that "I am of the flesh, sold into slavery under sin" (Rom. 7:14), able to "will what is right, but I cannot do it" (v. 18), and "the evil I do not want is what I do" (v. 19).

He describes the cause of his inability to live a transformed life as "sin which dwells within me" (v. 20). Paul is not clear about whether he thinks of sin as an entity, separate from himself, that has invaded his body, overwhelms his spirit, and controls (still enslaves) him. This leaves a question whether he thinks of sin as a corruption of original sin inherited from Adam that redemption did not totally remove. Paul writes extensively, however, about the Christian life, applying both moral and spiritual principles in his guidance and admonitions:

- To Paul, the Christian life consists of being "transformed by the renewing of your minds" (Rom. 12:2) and as being humble, citing the example of Jesus as being humble in incarnation (Phil. 2:8).
- Paul instructs his readers to be caring in their relations with others, citing the guidance of the Decalogue (Rom. 13:8-10) and fellowship within the church (Gal. 6:1-2, Col. 3:8-9, 2 Cor. 2:6-8, Eph. 4:31-32).
- Paul calls on Christians to restrain physical temptations and practice high moral standards in life (Rom. 13:13-14, Col. 3:5, Eph. 5:3-4, Gal. 5:19-21).
- Paul sets forth instructions for stable family life (Eph. 5:22–6:4, Col. 3:18-21), unity within the church fellowship (Rom. 12:4-18; 1 Cor. 12:4-7; Eph. 4:3-4, 25-32), and civic order in society (Rom. 13:1-7, Eph. 6:9, Col. 3:22–4:1, 1 Thess. 4:10b-11).

Paul writes specifically about the role of the Holy Spirit in the transformed lives of Christians (1 Cor. 2:10b-12). He describes human abilities as being more than innate talents; they are gifts of the Holy Spirit, apportioned to individuals "for the common good"

(1 Cor. 12:1-11). Paul believes that the presence and gracious working of the Holy Spirit in a Christian's life is the source of personal characteristics and actions that he describes as "fruit of the Spirit" (Gal. 5:22-23).

Paul, however, is influenced by what he understands to be established correct social practices and theological tenets. He gives instructions about food offered to idols because of pagan sacrificial practices (1 Cor. 8:1-13). He writes about head coverings because he believes that, in both culture and religion, gendered hierarchies and practices are divinely determined and established (1 Cor. 11:3-16). What is to Paul an established belief in the immediate, or very soon, "return of Christ" (eschatological end time) is clearly reflected in his counsel about marriage or celibacy (1 Cor. 7:1-40). Paul's belief in election/predestination leads to his admonition to remain in "the condition in which you were called" (1 Cor. 7:20-24), while still giving permission for slaves to gain freedom if possible (v. 21).

Paul reveals himself in his writings as coming to faith in the post-incarnation development of the Christian movement. He brings his pre-incarnate tenets of Jewish belief and messianic hope with him. By his preaching, practice and writing, Paul establishes in early Christian faith some tenets of faith that are not found in the gospel records of Jesus' life and teachings. Some of them are significantly different. This problem in biblical exposition is not widely included in traditional tenets of faith.

Chapter 7

Learning from the Later New Testament Writings

Before the New Testament was canonized in 367 CE, many "Christian" writings were produced. Before there was a "sacred book," the doctrines of the faith were being set forth, discussed, debated, analyzed, and tested in churches. The Gospels and the Letters of Paul were cherished in the churches as most helpful for use in worship and teaching. From among the many that were written, a few were believed to be sufficiently inspired or apostolic to be included in the group that were canonized.

The post-Pauline General Epistles (written 65–150 CE) include The Pastoral Epistles, Hebrews, James, 1 and 2 Peter, the Johannine letters, Jude, and Revelation.

The Pastoral Epistles

The Pastorals (Timothy and Titus) are ascribed to Paul but are widely believed to have come from disciples of his, writing in his tradition. The tenets of faith described in the Pastorals are in harmony with Paul's letters, but the organization of churches and the emphasis on orthodox faith seem to be from a generation later than Paul. A dating for the Pastorals at 100–120 CE is appropriate.

Hebrews

Hebrews is unique among New Testament documents. It became attributed to Paul in Alexandria during the 1st century CE, but there has never been wide agreement about its author or time and place of writing. The writer seems to establish that animal sacrifice is no longer needed, having been surpassed by the divine and eternal sacrifice of Jesus. This emphasis seems to indicate that the writing was completed before the destruction of the Temple in 70 CE, while animal sacrifice was still being practiced.

The faith focus of Hebrews is a detailed description of the writer's belief that Jesus fulfilled the Jewish messianic hope by becoming the divine sacrificial blood offering to expiate the human guilt of original sin inherited from Adam's fall in Eden (9:12-14; 10:1-4,12).

The writer uses the Jewish priestly hierarchy to affirm the excellence of Jesus, declaring Jesus to be "much superior to angels" (1:4). He is described as a "faithful high priest" (2:17), who has a more excellent ministry (8:6). He has no need to offer sacrifice for himself (7:27), but he can and does "make a sacrifice of atonement for the sins of the people" (2:17) when "once for all he offered himself" (7:27). This perfect sacrifice is described as being offered in a "greater and perfect tent, not made with hands," when "he entered once for all into the Holy Place (heavenly), ... with his own blood, thus obtaining eternal redemption" (9:11-13).

The writer affirms the incarnate ministry and death of Jesus (2:9, 10:19-20, 12:2, 13:12), but focuses more prominently on how Jesus fulfills the messianic role of Christ (3:1, 4:14, 8:6, 9:24). The effect of faith, or non-faith, is cited in the writing about the wilderness experience of Israel (3:18, 4:2). Near the end of Hebrews, a great herald of encouragement to faith is set forth (10:19-11:40), and a graphic affirmation of Christian hope is offered (12:22-24).

James

The book of James is written in the form of a letter but not addressed to an identified specific group; it is sent to "the twelve tribes in the Dispersion." James focuses more on spiritual morality in Christian living than on doctrine or dogma. Since James is a very common name, there is no certainty about which James is the writer. He is widely believed to be the half-brother of Jesus, however. The letter is thought to have come from sometime in the last two decades of the 1st century.

James is best known for the faith/life relationship of teaching (2:14-26). This tenet is often cited as a contrast with Paul's emphasis on faith alone. The teaching in James seems to be more in accord with the teaching of Jesus that "faith transforms life" or "faith has no authenticity." James clearly affirms the centrality of faith in the Christian life (1:6), and reiterates the teaching of Jesus that greatness lies in service rather than in status and wealth (1:9). An ongoing development of religious beliefs is reflected in James' teaching about temptation (1:13-15).

James echoes the teaching of Jesus that freedom of choice is innate to human personhood, and that temptation and sinfulness arise from within the human heart (1:14, see Matt. 15:18-19)—not from some outside source or influence.

In his teaching about Christian living, James warns about the danger of social caste affecting fellowship by partiality (2:1-7). He cites the importance of discerning and practicing excellent spiritual values in contrast to attitudes and actions that degrade life (3:6-18). For fruitful Christian life, James warns about the human struggle, but he affirms the purpose, presence, and help of God for those who aspire to life in harmony with God (4:1-10).

1 Peter

A pastoral letter (1:1, 5:1-3) deemed authentic to Peter (before his martyrdom in Rome during the Neronian persecution, 64–68 CE), but apparently dictated to Silvanus/Silas (5:12), 1 Peter is addressed to the "elect sojourners of the dispersion" in Asia Minor, and refers to "their behavior among the Gentiles" (1:1, 2:11-12). By contrast, Peter reminds them that "once you were no people" (2:10) and addresses them as "aliens and exiles"

(2:11). These descriptive words echo Paul's reminder to Gentile Christians that they had been "alienated ...and strangers, ... having no hope" (Eph. 2:12), but "... now in Christ ... (they are) members of the household of God" (Eph. 2:13, 19).

Central to the religious beliefs in 1 Peter is the writer's sharing with Paul that the crucifixion and resurrection of Jesus perfectly fulfill the Jewish belief in redemption by substitute sacrificial blood expiation of sinful guilt (1:18-19). This divine fulfillment, according to that belief, is a destined plan from the "foundation of the world," and brought to pass in the death of Jesus by crucifixion (1:20). Paul and Peter and other early Christians declare that the resurrection of Jesus is the expression of God's gracious mercy, the source of Christian hope (1 Pet. 1:3, Rom. 1:4). The resurrection of Jesus is believed to be confirmation of the expiating and justifying sacrifice made by his crucifixion.

Guidance about Christian living is included in the writings of Peter, as with Paul, but neither cites the teachings of Jesus as the source for their admonitions. Peter does, however, use the "language of Jesus," familiar from the traditions written in the Gospels, quite freely in his writing.[1]

Peter reflects the early expectation among Christians that the eschaton, the "return" of Jesus to establish the kingdom, would come soon (1:5, 13; 4:7). He urges his readers to expect suffering (4:12-19), and encourages them to trust God and remain faithful. Peter warns the people to be on guard against the peril of evil, as "... your adversary the devil prowls around ..." (5:8-9). This reflects belief in moral dualism, one source of good (God) and another source of evil (an adversary of God, Satan).

Peter refers to the developing practice of Christian baptism, describing it as "being saved by water"—corresponding to salvation in the ark in the Noahic flood. He interprets baptism to be an "appeal to God" for "a good conscience" based on the "resurrection of Jesus Christ" (3:21). This tenet reflects a kinship with Paul's death-and-resurrection meaning of baptism.

One passage requires careful consideration. Following the crucifixion, Peter writes that Christ ... was "made alive in the spirit" and that "...he went and made a proclamation to the spirits in prison..." (3:18-19). This passage is described as the darkest and most difficult one in the New Testament.[2] The tenet of faith is believed widely enough that it is included in the familiar Apostles' Creed.

The creedal statement "he descended into hell," from early Latin editions, is more correctly written as "he descended to the dead" in some modern editions. The faith being affirmed by Peter is that Jesus as "living spirit," during the time after his death on the cross and before the resurrection, went to the "place of the dead" and preached to "spirits" there.

Two tenets of faith raise concern. The first is a question about the gospel being "proclaimed even to the dead" (4:7). I have not found this belief expressed anywhere else in the Bible, nor has it become a tenet leading to widespread practice in the Christian stream of religion. I am not willing, however, to deny that God may well "still reach out in love" after physical death to persons who have not before responded in faith. I leave that question with God.

The other tenet I find reflected in the passage is about Jesus being "living spirit" after physical death. The affirmation by Peter here accords with what has become a personal tenet of faith for me. I believe firmly in the existence of the realm of spirit. It is as equally "real" as the universe of matter. I believe as firmly that the soul is immortal and does not die when the body dies.

Jesus was "living spirit" after his body died. He was a fully functional person, alive in the realm of spirit. I cannot make any affirmation about "how he spent the time." Without the limits of body and space, time has no meaningful limits either. I find no reason to not believe that, as Jesus has "… gone into heaven" (3:22), at physical death we will also "as living spirits go into heaven - into the realm of God's presence."

2 Peter

Second Peter has been described as one of the neglected books in the New Testament.[3] It is thought to be the last written (c. 150 CE) and the last accepted into the canon (300s CE). It is not included in the Muratorian Canon (170 CE), but is included in the Athanasian Canon (367 CE). It has the form of a letter, addressed "to those who have received a faith as precious as ours" (1:1), but reads more like a homily than a letter.[4]

The writer has two primary concerns: false teaching and the eschaton. He begins by appealing to readers to keep faithful (1:3-8). He then affirms the inspiration of scripture and encourages readers to pay careful heed to them (1:19-21).

The false teachers being warned against are "among you" (2:1), using their presence in the group to deceive with their "destructive opinions … and… deceptive words" (2:1, 3). Specific identification of a "false teaching" is written in 3:3-7 as "scoffing" about beliefs concerning "the last days."

Tenets reflecting prevalent beliefs at that time are the fate of "fallen angels" (2:4) and warning about "backsliding" (2:10-22). The writer includes a graphic description of an "end-time fiery cataclysm" at the "day of the Lord" (3:3-13).

The Johannine Letters

First John is a much-loved and often-read general epistle. Although written in the form of a pastoral letter, the contents read more like a homily or a tract. Authorship was early and long believed to be the disciple John, but has come to be considered the work of a later follower in the disciple's tradition. Its attention to false teaching and eschatological concerns indicate that the addressees are likely second- or third-generation Christians, from the early 2nd century CE in Ephesus and Asia Minor.

The letter reflects familiarity, or actual dependence, on the Fourth Gospel. Beginning with a proclamation that is akin to the prologue of John, it focuses on similar themes: "God is light" (1:5), and "God is love" (4:8). The centrality of light and love are described as vital to a Christian life (2:8-11, 4:7-12).

At the time of the letter's writing, false teaching has arisen within the group being addressed (2:18-19). The false teachers are apparently apostates who are denying that Jesus is the Messiah (2:22-23, 4:3). The writer sets forth tenets that are prevalent in late Judaism and are early established as Christian belief. Evil is described as the "works of the devil" (3:8-10), a tenet that developed along with moral dualism during and after the Exile. The illustration about Cain (3:12) comes from the early chapters of Genesis that were crafted into the Jewish traditions in postexilic Judaism.

From the early chapters of Genesis also comes belief in the "sins of the whole world" (2:2), which came from the "fall of Adam" in Eden. The tenet of faith about Jesus being "the atoning sacrifice" for original sin (2:2, 4:10) is a Jewish atonement belief applied to the crucifixion of Jesus, primarily by the preaching and writing of Paul and Peter.

Two tenets set forth in 1 John are problematic. The matter of sinlessness in Christians (3:6, 9), I do not find elsewhere. I have no basis for it, unless the writer means to describe our state as "forgiven," and I do not find this in the statement. Also, no description is written about the distinction between "mortal sin" and "not mortal sin" (5:16-17). Psalm 51:1 does describe three depth levels of sinfulness: "sin" (unintentional missing the mark), "transgression" (deliberate, intentional acts of evil), and "iniquity" (to think evil and practice evil to the extent the soul is so corrupt it can conceive only evil). The passage in 1 John gives no such detail of meaning, however.

Throughout the letter the writer returns to his encouragement to walk in the light and to practice love. He describes a Christian life as caring for others (2:10; 3:11, 16-18) and living by the commands of God/Christ (1:7, 2:3, 3:21-24, 5:2-3).

The Johannine letters conclude with 2 John and 3 John, thought to be circulars intended to accompany or follow 1 John. Although informative about context, they are not instructive about tenets of faith. Both are written by "the elder" and addressed to "the elect lady" and "the beloved Gaius," but there is no indication of whether the elder is a church official or a highly esteemed older layman. The elect lady (2 John 1:1) is believed to be a church and its members. Gaius seems to be a faithful layman.

Second John emphasizes the central importance of love (vv. 5-6), cites the problem of the denial of incarnation (v. 7), and warns about false teachers who wander from church to church (vv. 7, 10). Some internal division also has arisen (v. 9).

The three Johannine letters were early identified as closely associated with the gospel of John, and so are widely believed to come from Ephesus, or that area, in the late 1st/early 2nd century.

Jude

The 25 verses in the book of Jude read more like a tract than a letter. Jude certainly seems to have been intended for circulation among churches as warning and encouragement to "contend for" the faith that was "… once for all entrusted to the saints" (v. 3). "The faith" evidently means the teachings of the apostles, for they have predicted that false teaching and apostasy will come into the churches (vv. 17-18).

Jude was most likely written during the first half of the 2nd century CE. By the mid-2nd century it had become "associated with" 2 Peter, and by the end of that century was widely circulated among churches both east and west of Jerusalem. The Jude named as the writer does not seem of certain identification, but is thought to be Judas, the son of James (Luke 6:16, Acts 1:13), who is a brother of Jesus (Matt. 13:55, Mark 6:3).

The urgent reason for writing (v. 3) is that "ungodly persons" have "secretly gained admission" into churches (v. 4). It is believed that the "denial" of Jesus (v. 4) is the Docetism heresy that would not accept the reality of incarnation, insisting that the "Christ" nature of Jesus came by adoption at baptism and abandonment before crucifixion. That false teaching troubles the churches during the 2nd century.

The writer of Jude has two primary concerns: sound doctrine and upright morality (vv. 18-20; vv. 4, 7, 23). The writer seeks to expose and warn against false teaching, to plead for steadfast commitment to apostolic faith, and to encourage the high morality of godly living. The letter itself is best known and most appreciated for the beautiful benediction (vv. 24-25).

The Revelation

The last book in the New Testament is the most difficult one to introduce and to understand. Revelation describes itself as an "apocalypse," a revealing (1:1). Apocalyptic writings of Christian concern arose in Judaism in the mid-3rd century BCE and carried over into the Christian era. This literary genre is characterized by highly figurative language. Revelation, for instance, is organized in seven groups of seven visions, and uses numerology coding (9:5, 11:2, 13:5, 20:4-6). Literary apocalypses were occasioned by violent times and crisis situations, and often written in secret coded language and symbols intended to escape adversary awareness.

This New Testament Apocalypse is assumed to have been written in response to Roman persecution of Christians in the Ephesian region of Asia Minor during the last decade of the 1st century CE. The identification with Rome is seen in the beast (13:1), Babylon (14:8), and the forces of Satan (17:1–19:10). Apparently, Domitian persecuted the Christians because of their refusal to perform worship rituals and declare devotion to the Roman emperor and to Roma, the female divine personification of the city of Rome.

The document itself is intended to be a message couched in symbolism (1:9-16, 4:1-2). The coded revelation is preceded by a series of beginning letters addressed to seven churches in the Ephesian region (2:1–3:22). The letters focus on problems such as false doctrine, internal division, faltering faith, and apparent unconcern. During the generation since their conversion from Gentile faiths to Christianity, the writer believes there has developed significant decline in faithful devotion to the faith and life of Christianity, hence the danger of their forsaking the faith in the face of persecution. In the document, the rewards for martyrdom are described as reasons for, and encouragement to, steadfast faithfulness (7:3; 14:1-5, 14:13).

The tenets of faith that lie behind the apocalyptic drama are rooted in postexilic Judaism. The drama is eschatological, meaning it comes from a dual worldview of present and future. The present age is seen as based on the Genesis stories of origins (4:11, 10:5-6), centuries of "chosen nation" development (7:4-9), present era of conflict and suffering (6:12-17), and culminating in a cataclysmic end (16:16–17:2). A triumphal messianic future will be the result of divine vanquishment of evil. The entire vision is based on divine control of history.

This apocalyptic drama describes itself as prophetic (1:3, 4:1, 22:7). Treatment of the document has been divided from the beginning. Before canonization in 367 CE, writers gave more approval as apostolic and prophetic, but dissent was also quite prominent. After canonization it became established as inspired and authoritative.[5]

Two historic events changed the interpretative focus of the included predictions about things to come. In the generation of its writing the forecast events were believed to be the destruction of Rome, an imminent end of the age, and a messianic City of God established in Jerusalem. That tenet fit well into Jewish messianic hope.

But time passed and no eschaton occurred. Constantine legalized Christianity in the Edict of Milan (313 CE). Persecutions ended in the empire, and martyrdom ceased to be a fear for Christians. The New Testament canon of documents accepted as "inspired truth" developed through three centuries and, when it settled on twenty-seven documents, included Revelation

That canonic inclusion establishes its inspired status for most of the Christian movement. From that time on, the focus of "things to come" predictions is cast toward a future eschaton. Through much of traditional Christian belief and application, Revelation has been understood as inspired and literal end-of-time prophecy.

For Christian theologians, this document has continued to be highly figurative, mysterious in meaning, differently interpreted, and canonically disputed. I understand it to be rich in symbolic meaning, but neither literal in meaning nor accurate in eschatological prediction.

One thing is certain, however: The absolute center of the writer's faith is the dominant role of Jesus. As Messiah, Jesus is the lamb who opens the seals (5:5-10), the redeeming leader of the saints (14:4b-5), the host at the marriage supper of the lamb (19:9), the conquering warrior (19:14-16), and the reigning king (20:4).

Notes

[1] A.M. Hunter, "Introduction to First Peter," *The Interpreter's Bible*, vol. 12 (New York: Abingdon Press, 1957).

[2] William Barclay, *The Letters of James and Peter*, 2nd (Philadelphia: Westminster Press, 1960), 275. Hunter, "Exegesis of 1 Peter," 132.

[3] Ibid., 335.

[4] Albert E. Barnett, "Introduction to 2 Peter," *Interpreter's Bible*, vol. 12, 164a.

[5] Martin Rist, "Introduction to The Revelation," *Interpreter's Bible*, vol 12, 353b. (For more detailed study, see pp. 351-354).

Chapter 8
Learning from Post-Biblical Changes in Tenets of Faith

The early Christian movement and developing faith is influenced by many developments and personalities. It is important to have a contextual perspective on the first generation of religious reaction and recovery, and on the nascent emerging of a "new" stream of faith and practice.

Christianity, as it develops, is significantly different from postexilic Judaism and of pre-Incarnation. Jesus puts a new face on God, and reveals by his life and teaching a different form and purpose for religious practices.

The disciple group of about 120, according to Acts 1:15, is the nucleus of followers who are still together after the ascension experience. Because of their faith relationship with Jesus, his execution is fearfully traumatic for them. His living victory over death, however, gives them a revival of hope and sense of mission. Their sacred book of Jewish scriptures is no longer an authoritative guide for them. The Twelve (including Matthias), with their eyewitness experiences and memories, are their best guidance (before Pentecost brings the awareness that the Paraclete is with them). They have decisions to make: Do we go back to our former ways of life (see John 21:3)? What do the previous instructions by Jesus mean for us now that he is no longer present with us? And a question that has been debated ever since: Who is Jesus, after all? Early Christians have no one to ask, except God in prayer.

The Pentecost experience brings them a new perspective. They begin to live transformed lives as followers of Jesus and apostolic (sent) witnesses about Jesus. "Followers of the Way" becomes one of their identities (Acts 9:2; 19:9, 23), fittingly indeed, for they remember that Jesus said, "I AM the Way" (John 14:6). Christian living is a distinct way of life, involving faith and convictions about the meaning and purpose of life, and about the practices of conduct that give meaning and purpose to life.

Controversy develops whenever the Christians go into the synagogues, just as opposition has been so harsh by the Jewish religious leaders against Jesus. Christians withdraw (are driven out) from the synagogues and develop group gatherings in homes for worship and support, which grow into "house churches" (1 Cor. 16:19, Col. 4:15). We have more records about early developments in Christianity from the ministry and letters of Paul than from any other source. Much else is also happening in those first centuries. Many documents are written that are not contained in our Bible. The tenets of Christian faith are being "hammered out," and not everything goes smoothly.

"Followers of the Way" Become Churches

The first development with continuing effect is the establishment of recognized leadership within groups as they form. The Twelve Apostles are recognized as leaders because of their first-person relationship with Jesus (Acts 1:21-22, 6:2). The Twelve appoint six "ministry assistants," a role that later becomes the office of deacon (Acts 6:3-6). Elders are also recognized as leaders and are trusted for their wisdom and guidance (Acts 11:30; 14:23; 15:2, 6). As the Christian movement develops, with churches being organized in many cities, a need for recognized leaders grows. When Paul establishes churches, he appoints elders (Acts 14:23, 20:17). Deacons are also identified in relation to the church at Philippi (1:1) and in the pastoral letter of 1 Timothy (3:8-13).

Later, the office of bishop (overseer) becomes the primary office of church leadership. As a church office, it appears in scripture only at Philippians 1:1, 1 Timothy 3:1-7, and Titus 1:7-9. In church history, the office is central in the developing hierarchy of priest, bishop, archbishop, cardinal, and pope in the Roman Catholic Church.

The establishment of clerical function in church life is a significant factor in the development of religious leadership. Although Jesus instructs his followers to observe the memorial supper (Luke 22:19 KJV, 1 Cor. 11:24) and to baptize newly-made disciples (Matt. 28:19), he does not assign any officiant for those activities. Through the passage of time, baptism and the memorial supper become the two central rituals of Christian practice. Ordained clergy become the exclusive approved persons to officiate at them as ordinances, or to administer them as sacraments.

Ordination becomes established as the way persons are believed to be "divinely" anointed and approved for the clerical role, and authorized to officiate at the ordinances/sacraments. The apostles begin the practice of "laying on hands" to set apart religious leaders/ministers in Christianity (Acts 6:6). By the 4th century, it has become both faith and practice that ordained clergy control the life of the churches and are the exclusive officiants of Christian religious rituals.[1]

Hammering Out the Tenets of Faith

In establishing the tenets of the Christian faith, certain questions arise and have to be grappled with: Who is this Jesus? He died like other humans. But the apostles preach that he arose. The traditions written into the Gospels a couple of generations later all affirm that Jesus "presented himself alive" and then "ascended into heaven" (Acts 1:3, 9).

Questions continue to emerge and lead to a major development in Christian faith: What is the nature of Jesus and his relationship to God? The first General Council held by the church fathers (Nicaea, 325 CE) convenes over the question, "Is the Son of the same nature and equally eternal as the Father?" The Council agrees that, yes, the Son is the same as the Father.[2]

Learning from Post-Biblical Changes in Tenets of Faith

A second General Council (Constantinople I, 381 CE) reaffirms the agreement at Nicaea and expands it to include that the Holy Spirit is also "consubstantial" with the Father and the Son.[3] The Three-in-One Trinitarian statement about divine nature becomes confirmed doctrine in the West (Mediterranean basin) through the writing of Augustine ("On the Trinity," 400–420 CE).[4]

In the East (north and east of Jerusalem), John of Damascus sets forth the prevailing faith (*Exposition of the Orthodox Faith*, c. 754 CE), writing that "It is impossible to say that the three, ... although they are united to one another, are one hypostasis."[5] A single, universally-agreed, Christian faith has never become established.

Where does this leave us? I affirm two things: First, the oneness of God must not be violated—Jesus is clear about that (John 10:30). Second, human comprehension and human language are simply unable to reconcile the mysteries of divine nature, or the inter-relationships within the infinity of all that God is and God does.

Concerning language, the term "triune" is a hybrid word that is defined by itself. The word "trinity" is not formed as an English word until the Middle English era (1500s CE). Because of the insufficiency of human language, much of the historic, and contemporary, attempts to make the subject comprehensible is doubletalk—words that "turn back upon themselves."

The awesome and wonderful mystery is beyond human capacity to understand or describe. Faith should stand on the oneness of God. The manifestations and actions of Father, Son, and Holy Spirit should be for us assurance of the undivided love, grace, forgiveness, and beneficent aspiration of God.

Writings Become Sacred and Canonized

The inspiration and authority of scripture has been unquestioned by traditional Christianity. The meanings of inspiration and authority, however, have been defined and interpreted quite differently through the centuries. These features of cripture are matters of faith.

The question of how the "sacred" writings of the varied religions of humankind came to be written, and how they came to be considered sacred, is a field of study unto itself and far beyond the scope of this book. There is, however, historic information about how the Christian New Testament comes into being.

The documents affirmed as sacred Jewish scriptures are finally agreed on by councils meeting at Jamnia near the Mediterranean coast northwest of Jerusalem (90 and 118 CE). These are accepted and included as the Old Testament of the Christian Bible.

As the Christian movement develops following the death of Jesus, the "followers of the way" have to develop their own tenets of faith. An established canon of Christian writings does not become agreed on until Athanasius, a bishop of the church in Alexandria, Egypt, names the twenty-seven documents as authoritative for the churches there

(367 CE). Councils at Hippo (393 CE) and Carthage (397 and 419 CE) declare the documents to be the orthodox New Testament.[6]

The documents that become the New Testament are written as Paul's letters to churches (50–65 CE), the four Gospels (65–100 CE), and some general epistles from as late as 110–120 CE. Many other Christian writings are produced through the decades and centuries until the canon of twenty-seven is agreed on and declared established. Through nearly four centuries, churches get copies of documents as they are able. They evaluate the writings and use the most highly valued ones for reading in worship and for teaching the tenets of faith.

The standards used for evaluation are, first of all, whether the writing comes from the hand of an apostle or from someone taught by an apostle; and second, whether the writing contains an authentic sense of being inspired. Obviously, such evaluations are subjective and they vary widely in different churches. Canonization finally gives widespread sacred status. No original manuscripts are known to have survived.

Church Organizations Develop

Any group involving numbers of people needs organization to function well. In the first two centuries there is no overarching organization in the Christian movement. The era is often described as the little "c" catholic church (catholic = general, everywhere). House churches have elders as leaders. As churches increase, bishops are ordained as overseer in a local church, later as metropolitan overseers of churches in a city.

A group of leaders called the church fathers develops. Councils are held as these leaders try to agree on issues of doctrinal belief. After the Council of Nicea meets in 325 CE, the churches begin to become denominational. Groups of churches choose to follow a leader who teaches a tenet different than the larger consensus.

During the early Christian centuries, influences such as culture, learning, sophistication, and wealth are more advanced from Rome east through the Mediterranean Basin, Syria and Palestine, to Mesopotamia and Persia, than is true from Constantinople north and west through more primitive and pagan Europe. The most prestigious churches and monasteries are located in the East.[7] After Constantine gives his support to Christianity (311–313 CE), the Roman church advances. The churches in the East prosper until they are decimated by the pressure of the spread of Islam and the dominance of hostile regimes controlled by Islam.[8]

In the West, by the end of the 6th century, Gregory the Great with the help of the emperor, using Matthew 16:18-19 as his authority, is able to establish "the primacy of Peter" for the bishop of Rome and make his claim of papal status effective.

In 1054 CE, the patriarch of Constantinople makes a rival claim of ruling authority. The result is a division between the Roman Catholic Church in the West and the national Orthodox Churches in the East, an organizational division still in effect today.

In 1517 CE, a Roman Catholic monk, Martin Luther, challenges some corrupt practices of the Church, is excommunicated, and the Protestant Reformation begins. This movement leads to the formation and development of the variety of Protestant and Evangelical Christian denominations that currently exist.

By the end of the 20th century, non-Roman Catholic Christianity in the United States becomes post-denominational, leading to a decline in loyalty to the tenets of faith and practices of a particular denomination. Church choice seemingly becomes more focused on cultural concerns, charisma of church leaders, and programs for children and youth of a single congregation. Increasing secularization of society also leads to decline in general church participation.

New Tenets of Faith Develop

As the Christian movement develops, churches become more numerous, leadership for local churches is needed. The expansion and advancement of religious leadership lead to the development of new faith and practice. By the mid-3rd century, a tenet of belief in the priestly function of the ordained becomes established. The sacerdotal status is based on their "representing Christ" in the "sacrifice" of baptism and the Supper offered by them.[9] That tenet develops into an established position of the ordained as "ruler of the church" by control of the two rituals/sacraments.[10]

The continued elevation of believed status for the two rituals as sacraments leads to the belief that they make a permanent imprint on the recipient; that is, they change the very nature (ontology, being) of a person permanently (Council of Arles, 316 CE).[11] This tenet is one of the differing beliefs between Christian denominations, defined as the difference between "symbol" and "sacrament."

The form and meaning of baptism change. There is no defined historical record of the process or the meaning for the changes. The first and most formative statement about the form and meaning of baptism is made by Paul in Romans 6:3-4. Using the example of Jesus' death, burial, resurrection, Paul writes that baptism is a dramatic expression of death (to an old sin-life), burial of that "dead life," and being "born into a new life in Christ." The form, immersion, portrays this meaning.

The first change is in meaning. By the mid-2nd century, baptism has come to be believed to have sacramental effect. When properly administered by an ordained minister, it is believed that Christ through the act bestows forgiveness and eternal life on the baptized person. Dissenters have continued to disagree.

Next the form of baptism changes, from immersion, to pouring, to sprinkling. I have found no authorizing act nor explanatory reason, but conclude, from context and meaning, that the developing change results from sacramental meaning, necessity, and convenience.

The sacramental meaning requires the baptism of infants, and infirmed elderly, to ensure their salvation lest they die unsaved. Pouring is used of necessity, to cover the total body, when immersion is not possible due to infirmity, illness, or imminence of death. I have found no reason for reducing pouring to sprinkling except for the sake of convenience, or transition to metaphor of meaning. Infant baptism is believed to be made personal by catechetical training and confirmation after the "age of responsibility."

***

The Christian faith is a living faith. The world changed through the centuries from Abraham forward, and the Hebrew/Israelite/Jewish faith developed and changed with it. The incarnate life and teachings of Jesus brought a radical new direction to that former historic stream of faith. The Christian faith began as a movement with the first "people of the way" as followers of Jesus. As a living faith the "religious beliefs" of Christianity have changed as the Christian Church has developed, divided, grown, and served. The living story continues.

Notes

[1] Reinhold Seeberg, *Textbook of the History of Doctrines*, vol. 1 (Grand Rapids: Baker Book House, 1954), 182.

[2] B.K. Kuiper, *The Church in History* (Grand Rapids: Wm. B. Eerdmans, 1951), 56b, 58a. Seeberg, *Doctrines*, 216-217.

[3] Kuiper, *The Church in History*, 75ab.

[4] Seeberg, *Doctrines*, 237.

[5] Ibid., 236.

[6] Edgar J. Goodspeed, "The Canon of the New Testament," *Interpreter's Bible*, vol. 1. (New York: Abingdon Press, 1952), 67-68.

[7] Philip Jenkins, *The Lost History of Christianity* (New York: Harper One, 2008), ix, 6-7, 47.

[8] Ibid., 30-31.

[9] Seeberg, *Doctrines*, 182.

[10] Ibid., 184-185.

[11] Ibid., 319-320.

Conclusion

I have endeavored to outline the biblical text through the development of the Jewish and Christians faiths, beginning with their origins and following changes through the centuries since Abraham of Chaldea sensed a "calling" from God. I have shown what tenets of faith and religious practices meant to the people in the context of their culture and the state of information about cosmology, scientific development, and technology available to them.

I readily identify as a nontraditional theologian. My formal training is in biblical ethics and systematic theology, but I have transitioned into an analytical theologian. My central religious authority is the life and teachings of Jesus as these have come down to us in the four Gospels. My last personal assignment now will be to set forth some personal tenets in which I believe biblical records, and interpretations of them, have developed differently from what I believe to be the more authoritative revelation made by Jesus.

Sin and Salvation

Nothing is more important to us as individuals than our relationship with God. What we believe about that relationship centers on the subjects of sinfulness and salvation. I believe Jesus reveals a different meaning about salvation than the crucifixion-centered theology of Paul (see 1 Cor. 2:2). I will begin with a summary of the two tenets of faith: sin and salvation.

The most forthright words from Jesus on this subject are "Repent, and believe in the good news" (Mark 1:15, Matt. 4:17). Jesus deals with people as though we are sinful and in need of reconciliation with God. His teaching and practice reveal that we have the ability and freedom to choose and act on the basis of what we believe or don't believe, what we trust or don't trust, what we value or don't value, and what we are willing or not willing to do. These choices are described as loving darkness and doing evil (John 3:19-21) or following Jesus and having the light of life (John 8:12).

Jesus teaches that repentance is vital (Luke 13:2-5), and only a "birth from above," a spiritual transformation of life, can bring a person into harmony with God (John 3:3-7). Believe Jesus and follow him with a new heart; love the light and walk in it. God's loving grace, compassionate forgiveness, and life transformation are the divine actions that make reconciliation real.

Jesus does not teach a religion of good works or of following a good example. Jesus teaches a religion of faith response to the loving initiative of God who seeks "to save the lost" (Luke 19:10). A human response that leads to "new birth" and "life in Christ" involves a repentant turnaround in values believed and in chosen practices of life. A repentant turnaround in life will happen only when a person "believes the good news" enough to trust in God and make a life commitment to "follow Jesus."

A sinful person cannot make such a response without the conviction, enlightenment, guidance, forgiveness, and help of the Holy Spirit, who is God abiding with us (John 14:16). Such a transformation of life leads to "leaving the darkness" to "walk in the light" in reconciled harmony with God. That is what I believe Jesus reveals, teaches, and lives among us.

Now, about what Paul believes, as his recorded words describe it: Without question, he believes in "salvation through faith" (Eph. 2:8) and not by "works of the law" (Gal. 2:16). And Paul believes in the "grace" of God, a free gift by which God "justified" sinners.

Justified is a passive idea, that is, having something done for you. In religion, it means that God acts through a gift of grace to "redeem" sinners. In Romans 3:24-25, Paul wrote that Jesus was "put forward" to "be a sacrifice of atonement by his blood" (his crucifixion). The grace-gift of justification can be received by sinners through faith.

The texts that describe the crucifixion of Jesus as a blood sacrifice to atone for human sinfulness are found predominantly in the writings of Paul. The theology of Paul is written in most thoughtfully organized form in the book of Romans.[1] In that book he explains that universal human sinfulness exists, causing alienation from God, and unless "removed" by "the free gift of God," it results in "death" (3:23, 6:23).

The tenet of faith about universal sinfulness is based on the garden of Eden story about the disobedience of Adam and Eve (Gen. 3:1-24). Belief in the fall of humanity, original sin, and universal inherited curse did not become a tenet of Judaism until after the Babylonian exile (see Deut. 24:16, 2 Kgs. 14:6, Ezek. 18:20).[2] Paul wrote that the "curse" of sin results from the "original" sin of Adam (Rom. 5:12). The church fathers followed Paul to affirm and teach that tradition:

- Tertullian (2nd century CE) wrote that Adam's disobedience passed by heritage (the infection of his seed) to the whole human race.[3]
- Augustine (4th–5th centuries CE) taught that the human race is "a mass of sin" and that no one, not even newborn children, is free from original sin."[4]
- Martin Luther (16th century CE) penned that human nature is "a corrupted nature" and "from Adam down, the essence and nature of man is corrupt," that "through the act of generation, which is performed in evil lust, sin passes from parents to their children"; it is "inherited sin" so "the will is free only to do evil, but not to repent."[5]

In Romans 1:18, God's reaction to human sin is described as one of wrath. Paul affirms a belief that "sin came into the world through one man (Adam) and death through sin" (Rom. 5:12). In Romans 9:17-23, Paul refers to an "election to wrath" that precedes human disobedience.

In the developing doctrines of the church fathers, from Tertullian and Augustine to Luther and Calvin,[6] both the doctrine of original sin as the cause of human sinfulness and the doctrine of election reflected in God's molding "vessels of wrath" and "vessels of mercy" have been central in traditional Christian theology.

Paul described salvation as fulfillment of a divine plan, hidden in mystery until completed in time as revealed to him (Eph. 1:9-10). The plan began when God made an election "before the foundation of the world" (Eph 1:4). It involved the first man (Adam) who sinned and caused all humanity to be sinful and subject to death (Rom. 5:12, 15, 18; 1 Cor. 15:22). God elected and predestined some to be redeemed (Rom. 8:29-30). God "put forward" Jesus to be a "sacrifice of atonement" to justify redemption of the elect, "effective through faith" (Rom. 3:24-25).

This is the point at which, according to Paul, human faith comes into play. Redemption through blood and justification by grace are gifts to be received by faith (Rom. 3:25, Eph. 2:8). Salvation is received, and reconciliation is made effective.

How are the teachings of Paul and Jesus different? Grace and redemption are not words recorded to have been used by Jesus. Rather, Jesus spoke of love and forgiveness on the part of God. He called for faith, repentance, trust, and living by the guidance and help of the Holy Spirit by anyone who would "follow" him. The "way of salvation" revealed in the teaching of Jesus is: "believe the gospel, trust God enough to turn in commitment to follow Jesus, become a new person by a birth from above through the transforming work of the Holy Spirit."

Paul wrote essentially the same, except his writings reflect belief in a preceding necessity for God to fulfill, because of his loving grace: the vicarious substitute blood sacrifice by the crucifixion of Jesus to appease the wrath of God (Rom. 1:18, 5:9), wipe away the guilt of sin, justify opening the way of faith for sinners to accept that gracious free gift of God.

I understand that Paul's belief in the "atoning" necessity of "substitute blood sacrifice" came from his Jewish heritage and led to his crucifixion-centered theology. I do not find that tenet of faith in the teaching of Jesus. In his recorded words about his coming death (Matt. 16:21, 17:22-23, 20:18-19; Mark 8:31, 9:31, 10:33-34; Luke 9:22, 9:44, 18:32-33), Jesus did not even hint that his death would be an atoning sacrifice. As the records about his trial and crucifixion in the Gospels reflect, the reason for his death is the same as Jesus described: The Jewish religious leaders rejected him with violent opposition, and insisted that Gentile Pilate condemn and execute him.

Because of my deep devotion to Jesus as the most authoritative revelation by God to us, I cannot base my faith in the teachings of anyone other than Jesus.

Religious Rituals

Rituals are a part of our lives. We have family rituals, seasonal rituals, patriotic rituals, and religious rituals. Most of our rituals are so familiar and long established that we have not examined them carefully to understand where they came from and what they mean. Let's trace the development of some of our religious rituals in an attempt to understand them better and make them more meaningful.

Rituals of religion are activities that are considered sacred. They are either permitted or required as expressions of obedience to and worship of a deity. Rituals involve use of physical objects, in specific places, with defined actions. The practice of some form of ritual is almost universally established as part of every form of religion that has developed in the history of humanity.

The origin of rituals among most tribal religions known in association with the Jewish/Christian stream of religious development was associated with a place believed sacred because a deity inhabited it.

The earliest ritual recorded in the Bible is the practice of building altars and offering sacrifices on them (Gen. 12:6-8). The story about Noah (Gen. 8:20) was added to Jewish traditions after the Babylonian exile (see chapter 4, pp. 39-40). After the exodus from Egypt, the rituals of Israelite religion became centered in the Tabernacle, until the Kingdom era when Solomon built the Temple. Temple worship was central until the Babylonian destruction of Jerusalem in 586 BCE. Synagogue worship, without animal sacrifice, developed in Babylon/Persia. Synagogue worship rituals consisted primarily of Torah reading and prayers. Temple sacrifices resumed among the returning exiles in Jerusalem (Ezra 6:16-18), and continued until the Roman destruction of the Temple in 70 CE. (See the discussion of the Mosaic sacrificial system in chapter 2, pp. 25-28).

After the Incarnation, as the Christian movement began, the early Christians left—or were driven—out of the synagogue. As Christianity developed, the Jewish rituals were no longer meaningful. Rituals with specifically Christian connections and meanings arose, along with the development of the theology of the movement.

The first Christian rituals to develop were baptism and the memorial supper. The early Christians associated these personally with Jesus, and simply copied what they remembered from his time on Earth. At the beginning, apostles who had been present at the time of Jesus established the meaning of the rituals. Through the centuries those meanings have been debated, refined, and changed—first by the church fathers, and ever since by theological shapers of Christian doctrine. Additional rituals, later called sacraments, developed and became deemed as sacred until now we have the complex denominational doctrines and practices of contemporary Christianity.

The fundamental question we need to consider is what a ritual observance means to individuals in their practice of religion. Does a ritual mean what a person believes it to mean, and practices it to express that meaning? Or does a ritual have a meaning established by God and made effective by God when it is practiced as prescribed through a church?

The apostles and Paul, all of Jewish heritage, shaped the earliest Christian beliefs. According to their heritage, God established all rituals of their religion and required of

Conclusion

believers simple acceptance and obedience. It seems that the same belief about ritual practices was applied to baptism and the memorial supper. Paul said: "... all of us who have been baptized into Christ Jesus were baptized into his death" (Rom. 6:3), and "... if we have died with Christ, we believe that we will also live with him" (Rom. 6:8). Common features of apostolic faith about salvation are that baptism is a means of "begetting new life and bestowing forgiveness of sins," and that the memorial supper (Eucharist) is a "means to immortality."[7]

I do not find the feature of ritual to be prominent in the life, practice, and teachings of Jesus. The records in the Gospels tell of his synagogue attendance (Luke 4:16), but synagogue worship consisted of Torah reading, teaching, and prayers. Jesus spent time in the Temple, but while there was teaching the people (Matt. 26:55), not practicing rituals or offering sacrifices. I am persuaded, by the preaching of Jesus, that reconciliation with God comes by "repentance and faith" from a trusting person (Mark 1:14-15), which leads to a "new birth from above" (John 3:3-6) by the forgiving, transforming grace of God. No rituals are described as being required.

In my Jesus-centered faith, I believe rituals can have a helpful and enriching role. A ritual, such as baptism or even lighting a candle, can be a splendid vehicle for teaching about spiritual things. Once a spiritual meaning has become grasped by a believer, then any ritual can be a wonderful way of expressing worship to God, alone and in fellowship with others.

Now, about sacraments: During the first four centuries of Christianity, two significant developments took place. First, the church transitioned from being "the holy people of God believing in Jesus Christ" into a hierarchy of bishops (clergy), ruling the laity "by virtue of divine authority."[8] Successors of apostles became bishops, and later one bishop, claiming primacy from Matthew 16:18-19, became a pope. While the church was becoming more rigidly institutionalized, the beliefs about rituals were also becoming more specifically sacramental.

The Jewish practice of immersing Gentiles, who wished to become Jewish, to "cleanse" them of their "gentile uncleanness," included belief that immersion was an effective means of the cleansing. Paul applied the concept of death, burial, and resurrection to baptism (Rom. 6:1-4). His belief seems to be that the ritual is the means by which the "old life" is put off and the "new life in Christ" is raised to life. I find neither of these meanings in the teaching or practice of Jesus.

The early influence of Paul, through his teaching and writing, convinces me that his Jewish beliefs about the rituals of "immersion for cleansing of sin" and of "substitutionary blood sacrifice for atonement" were carried over by him from his Jewish heritage into his Christian faith. They are the foundation for the belief about rituals in Christianity.

Baptism and the Eucharist, as means for the bestowal of salvation and eternal life, became the dominant teachings of the church fathers and the hierarchical church going forward. Although dissenters were always present, they were overwhelmed and "cast out" by the developing hierarchy of clergy.

The ritual of ordination is another feature of the Christian movement that has its roots in the long-established priesthood of Judaism. After Aaron and the tribe of Levi were set apart and "sanctified" as priests (Leviticus 8–9), the "ordained" dominated the ongoing faith and practice of Judaism. Jesus chose twelve apostles—not priests—and sent them out to teach and do ministry—not do rituals (Matthew 10). When assistants for the apostles were needed, however, the Twelve chose to establish the practice of a ritual that was familiar to them from their Jewish heritage (Num. 27:23, Deut. 34:9). They "[laid] their hands on them" to "set them apart" (Acts 6:6). I believe, from that well-intentioned practice, the Christian clergy has used the vehicle of ordination to accept the role of ministry and service to and among God's people.

Tragically, it seems that ordination has been the vehicle that "Christian clergy" as an "office" has developed into a belief that the ritual bestows on an individual spiritual ability (gifts, charisma) that makes the ordained different from other Christians. At the Council at Arles (316 CE), Augustine set forth the doctrine that the "sacraments" of baptism and ordination "impress" on a man "an indelible character," a permanent character, that in the Catholic Church neither dare be repeated.[9]

In summary, behind and underneath all of the belief and practice of rituals and sacraments, there has always been belief, debate, and difference about the role of divine grace in relation to the ritual. Does the ritual bestow the grace, or does the ritual bear witness to the grace already received by faith, forgiveness, and commitment? Is the effect of the ritual permanent, or does the meaning of the ritual depend on the relationship of the participant and God? There have long been, and there will be ongoing, differences and debate about answers to these questions.

What makes a sacrament sacred? It is God's action. When God's Spirit touches a human spirit, in any experience, it makes that moment and that experience sacred. A ritual may be involved, but a ritual is not necessary. A ritual may be a vehicle to enable, but a ritual cannot be a means to cause the sacred to happen. A sacramental experience is between a person and God. It can happen when a person is praying, reading a Bible, even seeing an awesome sunrise or holding a newborn baby. A ritual can be a vehicle by which a person experiences a sacrament, or gives witness to sacrament already experienced. But a sacrament is always between a person and God, and it is always by God's action, not ours. I believe that baptism, observance of the Lord's Supper, and every ritual of religion should be practiced in a spirit of reverent worship of God, trusting his outreaching gift of sacred grace.

Conclusion

A Disclaimer and an Affirmation

I am keenly, personally aware, that what I have written in this manuscript is colored by my personal religious faith. I have tried to be carefully accurate about the information I have set forth. The interpretations and applications are my own, so I freely accept responsibility for them. My pilgrimage began with a "spoon-fed" youth about the meaning of the Bible. My journey has taken me through decades of searching, learning, reasoning, analyzing, and concluding. I believe deeply in the inspirational guidance and help of God's Holy Spirit in my life, as I trust it was present in the lives of all who went before me.

I have feared that some of the "differences" I have written about would "distress" the faith of some readers, but have dared write about them anyway for two reasons. First, I have become convinced that they are "true to the revelation by Jesus." Second, I have lived as an adult with a sense of divine calling to learn all I can about God and share the good news from God as widely as my life's opportunities make possible. If anything I have written "lights a candle" or "plants a seed" that helps anyone "see light more clearly," I approach the end of my journey with gratitude and fulfillment.

Notes

[1] William Barclay, *The Letter to the Romans*, 2nd ed. (Philadelphia: Westminster Press, 1957), xxi.

[2] Gerald R. Cragg, "The Epistle to the Romans, Exposition," *The Interpreter's Bible*, vol. 9 (New York: Abingdon Press, 1954), 462-63.

[3] Reinhold Seeberg, *Textbook of the History of Doctrines*, vols. 1, 2 (Grand Rapids: Baker Book House, 1954), 122-123.

[4] Ibid., 338.

[5] Seeberg, *Textbook of the History of Doctrines*, 242-243.

[6] Ibid., 398.

[7] Seeberg, *Doctrines*, vol. 1, 79.

[8] Ibid., 175, 177, 182.

[9] Ibid., 319.

www.ingramcontent.com/pod-product-compliance
Lightning Source LLC
Chambersburg PA
CBHW071010160426
43193CB00012B/1994